LEGACY OF

Blue

45 Years of
KANSAS CITY ROYALS
History & Trivia

BY

MARK STALLARD

FOREWORD BY JOHN MAYBERRY

**KAW VALLEY
BOOKS**

Updated Edition

ISBN-13: 978-0-578-13862-6
ISBN-10: 057813862X

Library of Congress Control Number: 2014934413

KAW VALLEY BOOKS
P.O. BOX 26242
OVERLAND PARK, KS 66225

This book was originally published under the title *Kansas City Royals Facts & Trivia*. This edition is an updated version of the original book.

Legacy of Blue is not an official publication of, nor is it endorsed by, the Kansas City Royals Baseball Club.

Contents

LEGACY OF

Blue

45 Years of
KANSAS CITY ROYALS
History & Trivia

To my little sluggers,

Walt and Nate

Foreword

by
John Mayberry

When I first came to the Royals in 1972, I never imagined that the franchise and city would become a big part of me for the rest of my life. I'd played in a small amount of games for the Houston Astros, but the Royals gave me a chance to play every day, and boy, did it ever turn out to be a great thing for me. I busted out and became the kind of major league hitter I always wanted to be, and more importantly, the kind of power hitter the Royals needed.

The early 1970s were an incredible time for baseball in Kansas City and around the country. I got to play with some amazing, talented ballplayers—George Brett, Amos Otis, Frank White, Freddie Patek, Steve Busby, and Paul Splittorff to name a few. Great players, even better teammates. The team got better and better each season, and winning division titles in 1976 and 1977 was a great thrill for all of us. I just wish we'd been able to go to the World Series while I was still in Kansas City.

I had many personal accomplishments during my time with the Royals—hitting a grand slam, a couple of three-homer games, representing the Royals in the All-Star game, and of course, helping the team win its first two division titles. All great memories. In 1996, I was inducted into the Royals Hall of Fame, truly a great and humbling honor. One of the best, though was when I hit for the cycle—getting a single, double, triple, and home run—in 1977. It was special to me then, and it's special now because hitting a triple was never an easy thing for me.

The 1977 Kansas City Royals won 102 games, the most in franchise history, but it wasn't an easy season. For the first four months of the year it looked like we wouldn't win the division. Then we won 10 games in a row in late August, and followed that streak with 16 in a row in September. That was more than enough, and we pulled away to win the title again.

When the White Sox came to Kansas City on August 5, 1977, for a three-game series, we trailed them by four and a half games, but we knew it was our chance to cut into their lead. In the second inning of that first game, I got a single as we scored five times. I led off the third inning with a homer as we scored three more runs to go up 8-1, which pretty much sealed the game.

But I was just getting started.

In the fourth inning I ripped a pitch into the right field corner, and I knew I could make it to third when Richie Zisk, the Chicago right fielder, didn't play the ball cleanly. I ran as fast as I could, lumbering around the bases, and for a brief moment I thought I might be able to get an inside-the-park homer run.

I rounded third hard and fast, and had to scramble a bit to get back to the bag. It was my only triple of 1977, and just the 13th of my career up to that point. My elation over the hit didn't last long, however, as I was thrown out at home when Amos Otis grounded into a fielder's choice.

I grounded out in the sixth inning, but when I came up in the eighth, I got another good pitch and laced a double into right field. As I stood on second base after the hit, the Friday night crowd of more than 38,000 fans was applauding and screaming loudly. Al Cowens had scored on my hit, but I couldn't figure out what else was going on. The Chicago pitcher was walking around and the rest of the players were not resetting to begin play. Finally, I turned and looked at the scoreboard, which was flashing that I had just hit for the cycle. So there you go. I was so into the game that I had no idea what I had just done. We won 12-2, then swept the White Sox out of town, and were on our way to the division title.

This book is loaded with Royals history and trivia, both good and bad, but it also shows a legacy of great baseball. How important were the Royals to Kansas City when I played? Well, we owned the town. Everything was blue in those days, and I'm hoping the city is ready for another long string of baseball in the blue.

Let's go Royals!

February 2014

Introduction

One of the things I like best about baseball is its history. It's always fascinated me how well-documented the game is, and studying all the different aspects of the game has always been fun for me, even rewarding. It goes without saying that I've studied the Royals a lot, warts and all. I have my own personal list of great Royals' moments that I saw in person, watched on TV, listened to on the radio, or followed on my phone app: I saw a World Series game in person, watched Brett's pennant-winning homer in 1980, listened on the radio as they clinched a division title, and more. I even caught a foul ball off the bat of U.L. Washington.

But of all the great moments in the Royals history, a couple of my favorites are ones that I missed.

In the spring of 1977 I was finishing my freshman year in college and trying very hard to compile acceptable grades. My first go around with finals the semester before had been sub-par, and I was determined to improve. So when I was offered a free pass to a Royals game two days before my hardest test, I didn't think twice about turning it down; I *had* to get an A on the final exam. Baseball could wait.

One of my closest friends, Mike O'Connell, took my pass instead. Mike wasn't much of a baseball fan, but he was always great at seizing spontaneous moments. He gladly went to the game, maybe more to heckle the players and drink a few beers. I stayed home and pretended to study.

I don't remember what I was doing when Mike returned from the game; maybe I was studying—though I doubt it—and more than likely I was watching TV or sleeping when he burst into the room.

"A no-hitter!" Mike screamed. "We saw a no-hitter!"

I thought he was joking.

"I'm serious," he continued. "Man, the crowd went wild and the team was crazy. It was the greatest game I've ever seen!"

I was stunned, couldn't believe my luck. Who threw it? Who was the pitcher? *But he couldn't remember the name of the Royals pitcher!*

Jim Colborn who had treated Mike to the no-hit gem against the Texas

Rangers, the first Royals pitcher to do so at Royals Stadium. And for the last few decades, Mike has occasionally mentioned the game and even rubbed it in a little.

"You know, I didn't really watch that much of the game."

But he'll also tell me how I'm responsible for helping him find joy in baseball, just because he got to see that no-hit game. I've always regretted I missed Colborn's no-hitter. Sometimes we make the right choice, only to find out later it was wrong. As for that test, I got a C.

Number two on my list of missed moments is the pitching duel between Bret Saberhagen and Nolan Ryan that took place in on a Thursday afternoon in June, 1991, at Royals Stadium. Once again, I'd been given the gift of tickets to the game, four of them, but I couldn't go. I had to work, so I passed off the tickets, this time to my dad, nephew, and brothers-in-law.

The game turned into a classic—of course. Saberhagen and Ryan were both great, but the game lasted long after they both quit pitching, lasted long after I left work. The Royals and Rangers played for 6 hours and 28 minutes (many of the 38,523 fans were gone before the end, including my family members), and Kansas City eventually won the game in 18 innings, 4-3.

"It was kind of boring," one of my brother-in-laws said of the game.

Another major miss on my part, but I probably remember it better by not being there.

The last 20 years have been bleak for the Royals—there's been very little for Kansas City's fans to cheer about, and there have been a lot of losses. A lot. Talented players were traded away for very little in return, and for seven years the team didn't have an owner. Somehow, despite the never-ending string of disastrous seasons, the Royals maintained a solid fan base, a strong following that has waited patiently for another winner. That time might be finally near.

More history awaits, but for now enjoy the dates, quotes, numbers, and names from the Royals' past. The good years were great, and the bad years were glorious in their awfulness. Hope, while fleeting and elusive in Kansas City, is still never far away.

Play Ball!

Royals History

George Brett and Bret Saberhagen embrace following the Royals' Game 7 win over the Cardinals that clinched the 1985 World Series.

True Blue Baseball
A Brief Overview of Kansas City Baseball

The past has become prologue. Years of losing, last-place teams and bad ownership left the baseball fans of Kansas City with a bad taste in their mouths. But it wasn't the modern-day Royals who did this to the KC faithful, it was the Kansas City A's, a team that was simply atrocious. And the A's weren't bad in a loveable way like the Chicago Cubs are, they were bad so that it was easy to hate them, hate their ugly green uniforms, their obnoxious owner, and that stupid mule. If ever a team deserved a city's contemptuous wrath and indifference, it was the Kansas City A's.

When Charlie Finley, the A's pompous owner, announced his intentions to move the team to Oakland at the conclusion of the 1967 season, it was a bittersweet thing for the city's baseball fans. The hated man was taking his hated team away, but he was also taking away Major League Baseball. Enter Missouri Senator Stuart Symington and Kansas City Mayor Ilus Davis. If Kansas City wasn't given another franchise immediately, Senator Symington threatened Major League Baseball, and then maybe an investigation by

Dick Howser, Bret Saberhagen and George Brett (all in Royals uniforms) talk about the 1985 World Series win with TV analyst Reggie Jackson and team owners Avron Fogelman and Ewing Kauffman.

Congress into baseball's antitrust exemption would be warranted. Mayor Davis simply threatened court injunctions to keep the A's in Kansas City. This double-edged political assault worked, and the American League promised Kansas City a new franchise for the 1969 season.

So Finley, who Symington described as "one of the most disreputable characters ever to enter the American sports scene," packed up his green uniforms and headed for the West Coast. And on January 11, 1968 the American League awarded Ewing Kauffman the new franchise for $5.5 million. Kansas City had Major League Baseball again, or maybe for the first time. It was a team worth waiting for.

Unions, Cowboys and Blues

Kansas City's experience with Major League Baseball before the Royals was not good, and that includes more than just the A's. In 1884, Kansas City got its first Major League team when the Unions were formed and admitted into the Union Association to replace the defunct Altoona club. A success financially, the Unions were horrible on the field, fashioning a miserable 16-63 record. But the club didn't disband until the league folded the following winter.

The city's second entry in the Majors was the Cowboys, a last-minute addition to the National League in 1886. This team was also very bad, and might have actually been worse than their 30-91 record. The long distances other teams had to travel and poor attendance by KC's unruly fans doomed the Cowboys. When Pittsburgh was accepted into the NL the following season, Kansas City was expelled. Attempts by the Cowboys owners to move into the American Association failed, and the team died.

The Blues were the third Kansas City entry into the Majors, entering the American Association in 1888 (the league was considered a major then). But like their two woeful predecessors, the Blues were a poor team and received shaky support. After the 1889 season, the Blues fell victim to the politics of baseball. After resigning from the AA, the team joined the Western Association, a minor league.

The upstart Federal League presented the last real challenge to baseball's Major Leagues in 1914, and included the Kansas City Packers. This team was mediocre and never really shook being compared to the minor league Blues.

The league itself suffered from several financial woes, and after losing huge amounts of money, the Feds folded following the 1915 season. Kansas City didn't have Major League Baseball for another 40 years.

The World Famous Kansas City Monarchs

Kansas City was without a Major League team from 1916 thru 1954, but they might have had something better: the Kansas City Monarchs, one of the greatest Negro League teams. Starting in 1920, the Monarchs played in two different leagues, operated as an independent, and had some of the greatest players ever wearing their uniforms. Pitching great Satchel Paige helped put the Monarchs on the baseball map, and while the Kansas City Blues of the American Association (minor league) were always excellent, the Monarchs gave the city a touch of baseball class only a Major League franchise could give. The demise of the Negro League teams came when baseball finally integrated in 1947.

The Kansas City A's

During their 13-year stint in Kansas City, the Kansas City A's were the worst team in the history of baseball, never finishing higher than sixth place (which it did only once). They finished last in the American League five times, never won more than 73 games in a season, and lost 90 or more games nine times. The great Satchel Paige pitched in one game for the A's in 1965—that might

The 1934 Kansas City Monarchs

be the club's top moment.

The best that can be said about the A's is that the team brought Major League baseball back to Kansas City. And then left.

Building a Legacy

For the first 25 years of their existence, the Royals were one of the most successful teams in baseball. They won six division championships, two American League pennants and a World Series championship. Success was a part of the franchise's tradition from the beginning, and for the better part of the team's existence, the Royals were a front runner in the league.

During the team's inaugural season in 1969, it was apparent this Kansas City baseball club was going to be run differently from former KC teams. The Royals won their first game ever, and by 1971 posted an impressive 85 wins and second place finish in the AL West. Smart trades (Hal McRae, John Mayberry, and Amos Otis) and good draft choices (George Brett, Willie Wilson, and Dennis Leonard) led to more success. The team moved into Royals Stadium in 1973, and by 1975 Manager Whitey Herzog had the club ready to challenge for a division title. The team joined baseball's elite the following season and won the first of three straight division titles. The American League Championship proved elusive, though, as the Royals lost to the Yankees three years in a row.

The team slipped a bit in 1979, but under new manager Jim Frey—with the help of George Brett's MVP season—the Royals returned to the ALCS in 1980. This time the team prevailed against the Yankees and brought Kansas City its first World Series. Although the team lost to the Phillies in the Series, it was one of the city's greatest baseball seasons.

Problems followed success. After winning half of the division title in

KC Shortstop Jackie Hernandez looks on in the Royals first-ever game as Jerry Adair puts a tag on the Twins' Rod Carew.

George Brett

1981, the team slipped to second in 1982 and 1983. But the club was able to revamp the pitching staff with Bret Saberhagen, Danny Jackson, Mark Gubicza, and Charlie Leibrandt. The Royals rebounded to win the AL West in 1984, and then produced the city's greatest baseball season ever with a World Championship campaign in 1985.

The Royals couldn't find the championship spark again following the World Series win. Manager Dick Howser left the team in the middle of the

The 1972 Kansas City Royals

1986 season when he was diagnosed with a brain tumor, and he passed away the following summer. The team still challenged for the division title almost every year through 1994, but was never able to capture another division title.

Losing

Ewing Kauffman, the club's only majority owner since its beginning, passed away in 1993, which left the team in the hands of its Board of Directors. In 1994, it looked like the Royals might grab a playoff spot, but when the players' union went on strike, the remainder of the season ended up being canceled, and the last realistic chance the Royals had to make the playoffs the past two decades was snuffed away.

Following the shortened '94 season, manager Hal McRae was fired, and Cy Young Award-winning pitcher David Cone and outfielder Brian McRae were traded.

The Royals have had just two winning seasons since.

David Glass purchased the club in 2000, and while his ownership provided some stability—the team was definitely going to stay in Kansas City—fielding good teams never seemed to be a priority. The strong tradition of winning, competitive ball clubs was replaced by a culture of losing: 100-loss seasons, last-place finishes, poor drafts, horrible trades, and unfortunately, a strong resemblance to their predecessors, the Kansas City A's.

There have been a few bright spots scattered throughout the losing seasons. The outfield of Johnny Damon, Carlos Beltran, and Jermaine Dye in the 2000 season was one of the best in baseball. The 2003 season was a fun joyride for Kansas City's fans as the team competed for the pennant into September. Zack Greinke was the top pitcher in baseball in 2009, winning the Cy Young Award in what was an otherwise dismal year.

Boys in Blue

The Royals' first 25 years are full of great moments: a World Series win, George Brett's batting titles, Frank White's Gold Gloves, Bret Saberhagen and David Cone's Cy Young Awards, and numerous division titles. But the winning tradition established by those Kansas City Royals teams in the 1970s and 1980s is little more than ancient history to the newest generation of fans. When Dayton Moore became the General Manager in 2006, the club took a small step forward. It has taken several years, but slowly the Royals have re-built the team from within. With 86 wins in 2013, the franchise finally appears to be on the cusp of returning to their true legacy of blue—winning.

The Royals celebrate at home plate following Justin Maxwell's walk-off grand slam in the final home game of the 2013 season. Kansas City defeated the Texas Rangers, 4-0.

Bret Saberhagen, Kansas City's two-time Cy Young Award winner, watches the final out of the 1985 World Series.

Royals Chronology
Day-by-Day in Royals History
1968

January 11 - Ewing Kauffman becomes the owner of Kansas City's new American League franchise.

March 21 - The Board of Directors selects "Royals" as the team nickname after a study of more than 17,000 suggestions from the Kansas City area fans.

April 25 - Free-agent Gerald Lyscio becomes the first player to sign with the Royals.

June 6 - Kansas City selects 25 players in baseball's Free Agent Draft, the first such draft for the Royals. The team did not have a first round selection.

July 11 - Ground is broken for the Harry S. Truman Sports Complex.

September 5 - The first season ticket drive is launched. First- day sales total an encouraging 2,156 season tickets.

September 9 - Joe Gordon is hired to manage Royals.

October 15 - Roger Nelson is the first player chosen by the Royals in the American League expansion draft. Other top picks include Joe Foy, Jim Rooker and Joe Keough. Future Hall-of-Famer Hoyt Wilhelm is chosen in the 25th round.

December 12 - Hoyt Wilhelm is traded to California for Ed Kirkpatrick and Dennis Paeke.

December 16 - John Jones is traded to the Houston Astros for Buck Martinez, Tommy Smith and Mickey Sinnerud.

Royals owner Ewing Kauffman speaks before the club's first game at Municipal Stadium in 1969.

1969

February 21 - Forty-six players participate in first-ever team workout at Fort Myers, Florida.

March 6 - Kansas City collects 16 hits but loses exhibition opener to Montreal, 9-8.

March 8 - Kansas City uses home runs by Pat Kelly and Chuck Harrison to win its first game, 2-1, over Washington, at Fort Myers. Roger Nelson, Dave Morehead and Jerry Cram combine to pitch a six-hitter.

> *They're spirited, clean-cut young-sters (one of the youngest Major League squads ever). Their attitude as a team is incomparably high. They help on another and cheer each other's successes.*
>
> **Ewing Kauffman, 1969**

April 1 - Lou Piniella comes to the Royals from Seattle in exchange for Steve Whitaker and John Gelnar.

April 5 - The Royals play their first game in Kansas City, an exhibition with St. Louis, but lose, 1-0.

April 7 - Season-ticket sales close at 6,805, a then all-time American League record.

> *One of the expansion teams will have the privilege of being the most successful franchise in 1969. Kansas City will probably be it.*
>
> ***Sports Illustrated's*** **Baseball Preview, 1969**

The 1969 Kansas City Royals

April 8 - Joe Keough's bases-loaded pinch single with one out in the 12th inning scores Joe Foy, giving the Royals a win in their American League opener against Minnesota, 4-3. Attendance at Municipal Stadium is 17,688. Moe Drabowsky notches the win for KC.

April 9 - The Royals and Twins play for 17 innings before KC prevails, 4-3. Tom Burgmeier gets the win.

April 13 - Mike Fiore hits the first-ever home run for the Royals, a solo shot over the right-field wall at the Oakland Coliseum.

May 4 - Bob Oliver goes 6-for-6 as the Royals pound the Angels, 15-1.

July 16 - Ellie Rodriguez becomes the first Royal selected for the American League All-Star team.

Bob Oliver

August 2 - Ewing Kauffman gives a commitment letter to Jackson County Court to lease the baseball stadium in the new sports complex. The lease is for 25 years, with an option for an additional 10 years.

August 26 - Omaha wins the American Association championship, giving KC its first farm club title. No other first-year club in modern history has had a minor league champion above Class B.

September 5 - Bill Butler K's 10 batters for the third time this season, but the Royals lose to Seattle 5-4.

September 11 - Ewing Kauffman announces plans for a Baseball Academy in Florida. Syd Thrift is named director.

Bill Butler

Lou Piniella, the 1969 American League Rookie of the Year.

October 2 - The Royals end their first season with a 69-93 record, one win shy of the modern-day record for first-year teams. They finish fourth in the American League West.

October 24 - Paul Splittorff is promoted to the major league roster, becoming the first player signed originally by Royals to reach the major league level.

November 26 - Sweet Lou. Lou Piniella is elected by the Baseball Writers Association of America (BBWAA) as the 1969 American League Rookie of the Year.

December 3 - In one of the club's greatest trades, Kansas City sends Joe Foy to the Mets for Amos Otis and Bob Johnson.

1970

January 20 - Ground is broken for the Minor League Complex and Baseball Academy in Sarasota, Florida.

April 7 - Opening Day in Kansas City. Amos Otis plays in his first game for the Royals, but the A's win at Municipal Stadium, beating Wally Bunker 6-4.

June 9 - Manager Charlie Metro is fired and Bob Lemon becomes manager. The Royals win 8-2 over the Senators.

June 13 - The Royals acquire Cookie Rojas from the Cardinals for Fred Rico.

July 1 - In another key move, Kansas City picks up Ted Abernathy from the Cardinals for Chris Zachary.

July 11 - Lou Piniella starts an 18-game hitting streak against Chicago. Bill Butler hurls a shutout as the Royals win, 4-0.

Amos Otis

July 14 - Amos Otis becomes first Royal to play in an All-Star Game. He plays the last six innings at Cincinnati. The National league wins the game, 5-4.

Cookie Rojas and Fred Patek

August 23 - Bob Johnson strikes out 12 Red Sox en route to winning 4-3.

September 21 - Jim York becomes first player originally signed by the Royals to appear in a major league game. His 4-2/3 innings of 1-run relief earns him an 8-2 win at Chicago.

September 23 - Paul Splittorff makes his debut for the Royals with a 6-0 loss to the White Sox in Chicago.

October 1 - Minnesota's Jim Kaat shuts out the Royals, 4-0, in the last game of the season. KC finishes with a 65-97 mark and another fourth place finish in the AL West.

December 2 - Another piece of the future falls into place when the Royals get Fred Patek, Jerry May and Bruce Dal Canton from the Pirates for Bob Johnson, Jack Hernandez and Jimmy Campanis.

1971

January 21 - The Royals' Baseball Academy is officially dedicated.

April 6 - Kansas City's Dick Drago beats the Angels 4-1 in the season opener at California.

May 31 - The Royals move into second place in the Western Division by sweeping a doubleheader in Boston, 7-3 and 9-4, and hold it the remainder of the year.

> *I want to do everything, so that when The Man (Ewing Kauffman) looks at me he'll want to pay me $100,000.*
> **Amos Otis, 1971**

June 7 - The Royals select an 18-year-old shortstop from El Segundo, California named George Brett as their second pick in the Free Agent Draft.

June 14 - The Royals win for the 12th time in 13 games as Mike Hedlund beats the Yankees 4-1.

July 9 - Freddie Patek becomes the first Royal to hit for the cycle. The Royals defeat Minnesota 6-3.

August 11 - Paul Splittorff throws a one-hitter in route to beating the Senators 1-0, in Washington.

September 7 - Amos Otis collects four hits and steals five bases at Municipal Stadium as the Royals defeat Milwaukee 4-3.

September 26 - The Royals win their 85th game of the season, a 5-3 decision over Minnesota in the second game of a double-header on the final day of the season. They finish second in the AL West.

Paul Splittorff

December 2 - Big John comes to KC. The Royals acquire John Mayberry and Dave Grangaard from the Houston Astros for Lance Clemons and Jim York.

1972

April 15 - A short players strike—the first of its kind—delays the start of the season. The Royals open with a win, beating Chicago at Municipal Stadium, 2-1 in 11 innings.

May 5 - The Royals trade Bob Oliver to the Angels for Tom Murphy.

April 23 - Roger Nelson comes within five outs of tossing a no-hitter against Boston. Ben Ogilvie's one-out single in the eighth is the only safety off Nelson as the Royals win at Municipal, 3-0.

April 30 - In a 16-inning affair, Cleveland defeats the Royals, 5-3, in the first game of a doubleheader. Al Fitzmorris takes the loss.

May 17 - The Royals battle Texas for 18 innings at Municipal Stadium before falling, 4-3. Ted Abernathy takes the loss for Kansas City. The game is tied for the longest in Royals history.

Roger Nelson

August 23 - Roger Nelson one-hits the Red Sox at Municipal Stadium. The Royals win, 3-0.

August 27 - The Royals drop another 16-inning game, this time to the Yankees, 9-8. Lindy McDaniel takes the loss.

October 3 - Jack McKeon is named manager for 1973.

October 4 - The Royals win the last game played in Municipal Stadium. Roger Nelson

Jack McKeon

beats Texas 4-0 with a two-hitter. Attendance is a mere 7,329. The Royals finish the year with a 76-78 record and a fourth-place finish in the AL West.

October 25 - Kansas City sends Jim Rooker to the Pirates for Gene Garber.

December 2 - The Royals make another great trade, acquiring Hal McRae and Wayne Simpson from the Reds for Roger Nelson and Richie Scheinblum.

1973

March 23 - Steve Busby hurls 6 innings and Doug Bird 3 to give the Royals their first no-hit game, a 4-1 spring training victory over Detroit at Fort Myers, Florida.

April 6 - Nolan Ryan beats Steve Busby as the Royals drop the season opener to the Angels in Anaheim, 3-2.

April 10 - Despite 39-degree weather, a crowd of 39,464 fans attends the inaugural game at Royals Stadium. Kansas City easily beats Texas, 12-1. John Mayberry homers, and Paul Splittorff is the winning pitcher.

April 27 - Steve Busby hurls Kansas City's first no-hitter, a 3-0 triumph in Detroit's Tiger Stadium. Busby struck out four and walked six.

Steve Busby

June 12 - Frank White makes his debut in a Royals uniform against the Orioles in Baltimore. Kansas City loses, 6-4.

July 24 - Kansas City hosts the 40th Anniversary All-Star Game. A then-record crowd of 40,849 at Royals Stadium sees the National League prevail, 7-1. Amos Otis and John Mayberry shine in front of the hometown crowd, collecting 3 of the 5 American League hits between them.

August 2 - George Brett is called up from Class AAA Omaha and at 20 years, two months and 18 days is the youngest Royals player to appear in a regular-season game. He singles in his second at-bat.

Frank White

September 3 - Joe Burke is appointed Vice President-Business and becomes a member of the Board of Directors.

September 26 - Paul Splittorff becomes Kansas City's first 20-game winner with a 6-2 triumph over the White Sox in Chicago.

September 30 - Kansas City is shut out in the last game of the season, 3-0. Steve Mingori takes the loss. The Royals finish their fifth season with a record of 88-74 and a second place finish in the AL West.

> *The turf should give us a lift because we play half of our games here...I think my range is as good as ever.*
> **Cookie Rojas**
> **on the artificial turf**
> **at Royals Stadium**

October 24 - Dick Drago is sent to Boston in exchange for Marty Pattin.

December 7 - The Royals trade Lou Piniella and pitcher Ken Wright to the Yankees for pitcher Lindy McDaniel.

1974

February 23 - The Royals obtain Vada Pinson from the Indians for Barry Raziano.

April 5 - Kansas City drops the season opener to the Twins at home, 6-4. Lindy McDaniel is the losing pitcher for the Royals.

April 6 - The Royals score a club record for runs in their 23-6 win over the Twins.

June 11 - Joe Burke is appointed Executive Vice President and General Manager.

June 19 - Steve Busby hurls the second no-hitter of his career in near-perfect fashion with a 2-0 win over the Brewers in Milwaukee's County Stadium. Busby strikes out three and allows only one base runner, a walk to George Scott leading off the second inning.

> *To me, the no-hitters are in the past. The one against Milwaukee went out when I got beat in my next game.*
> **Steve Busby, 1974**

August 6 - The Royals sign future Hall-of-Famer Orlando Cepeda to DH for the rest of the season.

August 27 - Hal McRae collects six extra-base hits in a double-header against Cleveland to tie a major league record.

September 14 - Paul Splittorff drops the first game of a doubleheader to Minnesota, 7-5. It is the Royals' seventh loss in a row, and 18th in their last 20 games.

September 26 - Steve Busby records his 22nd win, a 10-1 victory over California.

October 2 - The Royals lose 5-4 to the White Sox in Chicago to end the season with a record of 77-85 and a fifth-place finish in the AL West.

1975

January 24 - The Royals sign future Hall-of-Famer Harmon Killebrew after his release from the Minnesota Twins.

April 7 - Nolan Ryan beats Kansas City in Anaheim, 3-2, on Opening Day. Steve Mingori takes the loss.

June 30 - Veteran pitcher Ray Sadecki is picked up by the Royals from the Braves in exchange for Bruce Dal Canton, Norm Angelini and Al Autry.

July 1 - John Mayberry hits 3 home runs off Ferguson Jenkins at Arlington Stadium. The Royals still lose to the Rangers, 5-4.

Harmon Killebrew

July 24 - Jack McKeon is fired. Whitey Herzog is named manager of the club.

July 25 - Herzog's managerial debut for KC is a good one. The Royals beat Texas at Royals Stadium, 6-3, with Briles getting the win.

September 7 - Royals' DH Tony Solaita hits three home runs in a game against the Angels. KC wins, 8-7.

Tony Solaita

September 10 - The Royals and A's set an American League record by using 42 players in a nine-inning game. The A's win, 16-4.

September 26 - The Royals win their 91st game with an 8-6 victory over Texas, the highest victory total to date in Kansas City's major league history. Leonard gets the win.

September 27 - George Brett collects the last of his league-leading 195 hits. The Royals lose to Texas, 5-4.

September 28 - Kansas City ends the season with a loss to Texas, 3-1. They finish the year with a record of 91-71, good for second place in AL West.

John Mayberry

November 10 - Goodbye Killer. The Royals release designated hitter and future Hall-of-Famer Harmon Killebrew.

November 12 - Nelson for Nelson. Infielder Dave Nelson comes to Kansas City from Texas in exchange for pitcher Nelson Briles.

Whitey Herzog

1976

April 9 - Kansas City loses on Opening Day to the White Sox in Chicago, 4-0. Paul Splittorff is the losing pitcher.

May 13 - Brett sets a major league record by collecting at least 3 hits for the 6th consecutive game. The Royals beat the White Sox, 13-2.

> There was talent—good young talent—all over the place. I knew the team was going to win, and win a lot.
>
> **Whitey Herzog, 1975**

May 16 - In a trade that will reap big benefits for years to come, Kansas City sends catcher Fran Healy to the Yankees for Larry Gura.

May 18 - The Royals climb into the Western Division lead to stay with a 3-1 win over Texas at Royals Stadium.

August 9 - Largest regular season crowd (to date) in Kansas City baseball history—40,435—watch as the Royals record an 8-2 victory over the Yankees.

> George Brett may be the best all-around ballplayer in our league. And unless a bone is sticking out of him, he's ready to play every day.
>
> **Whitey Herzog, 1976**

August 17 - Brett steals home in the 10th inning to give the Royals a 4-3 win over the Indians.

September 4 - Willie Wilson plays in his first game for Kansas City as Dennis Leonard shuts out Texas, 7-0.

The 1976 Kansas City Royals, AL West Champions.

George Brett

> *I had by this time developed a considerable attachment to the spirited visiting nine, in their powder blue doubleknits, who had now twice come back to tie up this interesting series. Their veteran shortstop, Patek...was having a splendid time of it afield and at the plate...and the whole lineup, although clearly short of power...seemed to be crowded with youngsters who attacked the ball with great confidence and relish. Foremost among these, of course, was George Brett, had begun to look like the hardest out I had seen since my first glimpse of Al Kaline...*
>
> **Roger Angell**
> *Five Seasons*, 1978
> on the Royals in the 1976 ALCS

September 29 - Herzog turns to Larry Gura to break a four-game losing streak; Gura responds with a brilliant performance that clinches a tie for the Western Division title, winning a 4-0 triumph over the A's at Oakland.

October 1 - The Royals win the West! Despite losing to Minnesota at home, Kansas City clinches its first division championship when the A's lose to California, 2-0.

October 3 - George Brett edges teammate Hal McRae by .001 in a dramatic battle to capture the AL Batting title. Brett earned his first batting championship by posting a 3-for-4 showing and concluding the season with 215 hits, a league high and an all-time Kansas City record. The Royals lose the season finale, 5-3, and finish with a record of 90-72.

Hal McRae

October 9 - Game 1 of the ALCS (American League Championship Series) at Royals Stadium against the Yankees. Catfish Hunter tosses a five-hitter at the Royals, winning 4-1. Two Brett errors in the first inning hurt; Gura is the losing pitcher.

October 10 - Game 2 of the ALCS. KC evens the series at one game apiece with a 7-3 victory over New York at Royals Stadium. A Kansas City record (to date) crowd of 41,091 witnesses the win. Splittorff gets the win.

October 12 - Game 3 of the ALCS. New York wins at Yankee Stadium, 5-3. Hassler loses for Kansas City.

> *...George Brett, on the count of 0-1, socked a middling-deep, medium-high fly ball that landed just within the second or third row of the short right-field seats, for a tying three-run homer...Brett had confirmed himself a great hitter, for if ever a home run was intentional it was this one.*
>
> **Roger Angell**
> ***Five Seasons*, 1978**
> on Brett's game-tying homer in Game 5 of the 1976 ALCS

October 13 - Game 4 of the ALCS. The Royals even the series at two games apiece with a 7-4 victory over Catfish Hunter. Bird relieves Gura and gets the win.

October 14 - Game 5 of the ALCS. New York's Chris Chambliss homers in the bottom of the ninth off Mark Littell to send the Royals home for the winter—New York wins the game, 7-6, and the series, 3 games to 2. Brett tied the game in the eighth with a three-run home run.

Larry Gura

Frank White turns a double play in Game 2 of the 1976 ALCS.

December 6 - Kansas City sends Jamie Quirk, Jim Wohlford and Bob McClure to Milwaukee for Darrell Porter and Jim Colborn.

1977

April 7 - Kansas City opens the season in Detroit, stopping the Tigers 7-4. Splittorff records the win.

May 14 - Colborn pitches the first no-hitter by a KC pitcher at Royals Stadium, blanking Texas, 6-0. Colborn walks just one batter and hits another while facing only 28 batters.

June 1 - John Mayberry hits three home runs off three different pitchers in Toronto. The Royals win, 11-3.

July 2 - Andy Hassler tosses a one-hitter as the Royals defeat the Indians, 1-0.

August 31 - Jim Colborn beats the Rangers at Royals Stadium, 5-4. The win is the first of 16 straight for the team.

Jim Colborn

September 6 - Al Cowens bangs out five hits for the second time in 1977. The Royals win easily over the Mariners, 10-0, as Splittorff gets the win.

The 1977 Kansas City Royals, AL West Division Champs.

Al Cowens had a career year in 1977 with .312 batting average, 23 home runs, and 112 RBIs.

September 16 - Mariners beat Royals 4-1, ending Kansas City's 16-game winning streak, which began on August 31.

September 23 - Two straight! The Royals clinch their second straight AL West title with a 7-3 win against California. Dennis Leonard notches the victory for the Royals.

October 2 - Dennis Leonard blanks California, 2-0, for KC's 102nd win of the season, a club record and tops in the majors for 1977.

October 5 - Game 1 of the ALCS. In a rematch of the '76 playoffs, Kansas City takes the upper hand with a 7-2 win against the Yankees in New York. McRae, Mayberry and Cowens homer for the Royals, Splittorff gets the win.

October 6 - Game 2 of the ALCS. Guidry stops KC and the Royals lose, 6-2. The series is tied one game each.

October 7 - Game 3 of the ALCS. A 6-2 Royals' win puts KC up two games to

> *I can't believe we lost. There is no way that team over there (Yankees) should beat us.*
> **Freddie Patek**
> after losing Game 5
> of the 1977 ALCS

one. Leonard holds the Yanks to four hits in a complete-game victory at Royals Stadium.

October 8 - Game 4 of the ALCS. New York evens things up with a 6-4 win. Gura takes the loss.

October 9 - Game 5 of the ALCS. Ouch! For the second year in a row the Yankees win the AL pennant in the ninth inning of the final game, this time scoring three runs and winning, 5-3. Leonard takes the loss.

> *Just can't believe it. After we got them out in the eighth, I thought we'd be in.*
> **Frank White**
> after losing Game 5
> of the 1977 ALCS

> *The big difference between us and the Yankees in the two play-offs was...Sparky Lyle, and I had nobody nearly that effective.*
> **Whitey Herzog**
> on the 1976 and 1977 ALCS

December 9 - The Royals trade for Al Hrabosky, sending Mark Littell and Buck Martinez to St. Louis for the colorful closer.

George Brett slides in safely at third base with a triple in Game 5 of the 1977 ALCS and receives a kick from Yankees third baseman Graig Nettles. Brett retaliated with a swing at Nettles as Royals' third base coach Joe Hiller and umpire Marty Springstead look on. The fight started a bench-clearing brawl between the two teams.

Freddie Patek, Whitey Herzog and Darrell Porter discuss strategy with Paul Splittorff during Game 5 of the 1977 ALCS.

1978

March 20 - KC rookie Clint Hurdle is pictured on the cover of Sports Illustrated. The magazine ballyhoos the young player as a "can't miss" prospect.

April 8 - The Royals drop the season opener at Cleveland, 8-5. Dennis Leonard takes the loss.

May 8 - Birth of the "Herzog Shift." Royals Manager Whitey Herzog positions four players in the outfield at Fenway Park, leaving the second base area empty in an attempt to stifle Jim Rice's productivity. The shift fails as the Red Sox prevail, 8-4.

June 1 - Jim Colborn is traded to the Mariners for Steve Braun.

June 4 - Darrell Porter raps out five hits against the White Sox at Royals Stadium. Kansas City thrashes Chicago, 13-2.

Al Hrabosky

30

July 21 - Paul Splittorff shuts out Boston 9-0 for his 100th career win.

July 25 - The Royals lose to the Yankees at Royals Stadium, ending their 10-game win streak.

September 26 - Gura beats the Mariners 4-1 and the Royals clinch AL West for the third straight year.

October 1 - Kansas City wins the regular season finale against Minnesota, 1-0, and finishes with a record of 92-70.

Clint Hurdle

October 3 - Game 1 of the ALCS. For the third straight year, the Royals face the Yankees. New York raps out 16 hits and wins the opener, 7-1.

October 4 - Game 2 of the ALCS. The Royals collect 16 hits and rout the Yankees, 10-4, at Royals Stadium. Gura gets the win.

If I'd done everything I was supposed to, I would be leading the league in home runs, have the highest batting average, have given $1,000 to the cancer fund and have married Marie Osmond.
Clint Hurdle

Royals' manager Whitey Herzog and Yankees' manager Bob Lemon meet before Game 1 of the 1978 ALCS.

October 6 - Game 3 of the ALCS. George Brett hits three homers off Catfish Hunter at Yankee Stadium; still, the Royals lose, 6-5. Thurman Munson's eighth inning home run gives the Yanks the win. Doug Bird takes the loss for KC.

October 7 - Game 4 of the ALCS. For the third year in a row the Royals lose the AL pennant to the Yankees. New York wins, 2-1. Leonard loses his second game of the series.

> *We've got quite a rivalry going here.*
>
> **Paul Splittorff**
> during the 1978 ALCS

1979

April 5 - The Royals rout the Blue Jays at Royals Stadium on Opening Day, 11-2. Dennis Leonard gets the win.

May 28 - After 16 innings, the Royals prevail over the Orioles at Royals Stadium. Larry Gura gets the win in relief.

June 13 - George Scott comes to Kansas City from the Red Sox in exchange for Tom Poquette.

June 15 - After falling behind 11-2, the Royals rally to beat the Brewers 14-11 at Milwaukee. Willie Wilson becomes the first Royal to hit a homer from both sides of the plate in a game. Steve Mingori gets the win.

August 29 - Royals beat Brewers in 18-8 as Milwaukee's third baseman Sal Bando and former Royals' catcher Buck Martinez pitch.

September 21 - U. L. Washington hits a home run from both sides of the plate as the Royals clobber the A's, 13-4.

Willie Wilson

September 30 - Willie Wilson finishes the season with 83 steals, tops in the American League. The Royals lose the season finale to Oakland, 6-5, and finish the year with an 85-77 record, three games back of the Angels.

October 2 - The Royals fire manager Whitey Herzog.

October 24 - Jim Frey replaces Herzog as the Royals manager.

December 6 - The Royals acquire Willie Aikens and Rance Mulliniks from the Angels for Todd Cruz, Al Cowens and Craig Eaton.

Jim Frey

1980

April 10 - Detroit drops the Royals on Opening Day in KC, 5-1. Dennis Leonard takes the loss.

April 30 - Larry Gura pitches a one-hitter for his third shutout in five starts. The Royals win, 3-0.

May 4 - Darrell Porter returns to the starting lineup after spending six weeks in a drug and alcohol rehabilitation center. He drives in 3 runs in the Royals' 5-3 win over Boston at Royals Stadium.

May 7 - The Royals bang out 9 consecutive hits (one short of the AL record set by Boston in 1901) in an 8-run 4th inning. They beat the White Sox, 8-4, in Chicago.

May 14 - Royals' pitchers issue 14 walks in a 16-3 loss to the Yankees.

June 11 - Dennis Leonard pitches a shutout against the Indians in Cleveland, 5-0. The win is the eighth in a row for the Royals.

July 26 - A record crowd of 41,860 fans at Royals Stadium watch the Royals lose to the Yankees, 5-4.

August 17 - George Brett goes 4-for-4 against Toronto at Royals Stadium, pushing his season batting average over .400.

August 19 - Brett's 30-game hitting streak comes to an end. He batted .467 with seven game-winning RBIs before being stopped by Jon Matlack of the Texas Rangers at Arlington Stadium. The Royals still win, 4-3.

Dennis Leonard

August 17, 1980. George Brett stands triumphantly at second base after hitting a double to push his batting average above .400.

September 17 - Leonard shuts out Angels in Kansas City, 5-0. The Royals wrap up the AL West, their fourth title in five years.

September 18 - Willie Wilson steals second and third base in the 2nd inning against the Angels, an AL-record 28th consecutive steal without getting caught. The Royals win, 5-2.

October 4 - Willie Wilson becomes the first player in major league history to be credited with 700 at-bats in one season. He also sets the mark for the most singles in a season, 183, and becomes only the second player in history to collect 100 hits from each side of the plate. Brett goes 2-for-4 at Royals Stadium to finish the year with a .390 batting average and wins his second AL Batting Championship. Kansas City pounds the Twins, 17-1, as Leonard wins his 20th game of the year.

October 5 - Splittorff shuts out the Twins, 4-0, and the Royals finish the season with a 97-65 record.

October 8 - Game 1 of the ALCS. For the 4th time in 5 seasons, the Royals and Yankees meet to determine the AL Champion. Gura pitches a great game and Brett homers at Royals Stadium. Royals win, 7-2.

The 1980 Kansas City Royals, American League Champions.

The pennant-winning home run. George Brett hammers a 98 mph fastball from the Yankees' Goose Gossage for a three-run shot in the top of the seventh inning of Game 3 of the 1980 ALCS. The homer propelled the Royals to their first World Series.

October 9 - Game 2 of the ALCS. Kansas City take a two-game-to-none advantage, winning a squeaker, 3-2. Leonard wins with help from Quiz and Brett's relay throw to catch Willie Randolph at the plate late in the game.

October 10 - Game 3 of the ALCS. The Royals win the pennant! George Brett's three-run homer off Goose Gossage in the seventh inning gives the Kansas City Royals their first American League Championship and sends them to the team and city's first World Series. Quisenberry pitches big and gets the win in relief, 4-2.

> *I'm not even thinking about the World Series. I'll worry about that in another day or two. This day has been too long coming to think about anything else.*
> **Paul Splittorff**
> on winning the 1980 ALCS

October 14 - World Series Game 1. The Royals can't hold a four-run lead as the Phillies win an exciting game, 7-6. Aikens homers twice and Leonard takes the loss in Philadelphia.

October 15 - World Series Game 2. Brett is forced out of the game in the 6th inning with a severe case of hemorrhoids. Philadelphia comes from behind again, winning 6-4. October 16 - Brett has minor surgery for hemorrhoids.

October 17 - World Series Game 3. Willie Aikens' 10th-inning single gives the Royals a 4-3 win in Game 3 for the first World Series triumph in Kansas City's history. Back in the lineup, Brett goes 2-for-4 with a homer.

Willie Aikens

October 18 - World Series Game 4. Willie Aikens hits two more home runs as the Royals tie the Series at two games apiece, winning 5-3. Dennis Leonard gets the win with relief help from Quisenberry.

October 19 - World Series Game 5. Once again the Phillies stage a rally and win. After giving up 2 runs in the top of the 9th, the Royals load the bases, only to fall short when Jose Cardenal strikes out. Phillies win, 4-3. The series shifts back to Philadelphia with Kansas City down, 3 games to 2.

October 21 - World Series Game 6. Steve Carlton pitches the Phillies to the championship, beating the Royals, 4-1. Rich Gale takes the loss for KC.

Jose Cardenal strikes out to end Game 5 of the 1980 World Series.

November 18 - George Brett is named the American League MVP for the 1980 season. His .390 batting average is the highest since Ted Williams hit .406 in 1941. Brett added 24 homers and 118 RBIs to go with his impressive batting average.

All my problems are behind me.
George Brett
on his hemorrhoids
during the 1980 World Series

1981

January 21 - Cesar Geronimo comes to the Royals from Cincinnati in exchange for German Barranca.

April 10 - Kansas City drops the season opener to the Orioles at Baltimore, 5-3. Gura is tagged with the loss.

April 30 - The Royals lose to the Rangers, 7-0, dropping their record to 3-10.

May 22 - The Twins blank the Royals, 7-0. The Royals record falls to 9-22.

June 12 - The Major League Baseball Players Association goes on strike against major league owners. Games will not resume until August.

August 10 - The players strike ends and the 1981 second season begins. The Royals lose to Baltimore in 12 innings, 3-2.

August 12 - Frank White hits a grand slam as the Royals defeat the Orioles in Baltimore, 10-0.

August 31 - Dick Howser replaces Jim Frey as manager.

October 5 - The Royals shut out the Indians at Cleveland, 9-0, clinching the second-half AL West title. Splittorff records the win. The second game of the scheduled doubleheader is canceled. Because of the strike, a divisional playoff will determine the winner of the AL West. The Royals will meet first-half winner Oakland in a best-of-five series. KC's combined record for the year is 50-53.

Dick Howser

October 6 - Game 1 of the Western Division Playoff. The Royals are shut out at home by Oakland, 4-0. Leonard loses as KC manages only 4 hits.

October 7 - Game 2 of the Western Division Playoff. Oakland scores a run in the top of the eighth and hangs on to win, 2-1. The A's lead the series 2 games to none.

October 9 - Game 3 of the Western Division Playoff. The A's sweep the Royals by winning at Oakland, 4-1, to capture the American League West title.

December 11 - The Royals send Clint Hurdle to the Reds for Scott Brown. In another trade, Rich Gale and Bill Laskey go to the Giants for Jerry Martin.

December 21 - Mike Jones, the Royals' standout rookie pitcher in the 1981 season, crashes his car near Rochester, New York. Jones doesn't pitch again in the majors until 1984 due injuries sustained in the accident.

John Wathan and George Brett talk with Mike Jones in the 1981 playoffs.

1982

March 2 - Kansas City picks up Buddy Black from the Mariners for Manny Castillo.

March 24 - Greg Pryor is acquired from the White Sox for Jeff Schattinger.

> *It was the kind of year that you'd like to forget.*
>
> **George Brett**
> on the 1981 season

March 30 - A trade that will have major implications for KC in the next several seasons—Vida Blue and Bob Tufts come to Kansas City from the Giants for Atlee Hammaker, Renie Martin, Brad Wellman, and Craig Chamberlain.

April 5 - The Royals get hammered at Baltimore, 13-5, in the season opener. Dennis Leonard takes the loss.

May 16 - Hal McRae collects the 1,500th base hit of his career.

July 6 - Hal McRae hits a grand slam as the Royals defeat Boston, 6-2.

August 3 - Frank White hits for the cycle as the Royals top the Tigers in Kansas City, 6-5.

> *I'm not much on sour grapes. I think of the season only in terms of game 1 through 162—not one incident, one loss, one call or one player move.*
>
> **Dick Howser**
> on the 1982 season

August 24 - John Wathan steals his 31st base of the season in the Royals' 5-3 win over the Rangers. The theft breaks the single-season record for catchers set by Ray Schalk in 1916. Wathan will finish the season with 36 stolen bases.

October 3 - Willie Wilson wins the American League batting title on the last day of season, finishing with a .332 average. Hal McRae finishes the season with 133 RBIs, tops in the American League. The Royals lose to Oakland, 6-3, and finish the year at 90-72, second in the AL West.

John Wathan

1983

February 4 - The Royals trade Cecil Fielder to the Blue Jays for Leon Roberts.

April 4 - The Royals beat the Orioles 7-2 in Baltimore to open the season. Larry Gura gets the win.

George Brett hits one at Royals Stadium.

April 20 - George Brett wallops three home runs and drives in seven runs to lead the Royals to an 8-7 win over Detroit at Tiger Stadium. Quisenberry get the win in relief.

June 7 - Kansas City sends Bob Tufts to the Reds for Charlie Leibrandt.

July 24 - The Royals and Yankees become involved in one of the great controversies in baseball history—the "Pine Tar" game. With two out in the top of the ninth at Yankee Stadium, George Brett hits a two-run homer off Goose Gossage to give the Royals a 5-4

Gaylord Perry

lead. At the request of Yankee manager Billy Martin, home plate umpire Tim McClelland checks Brett's bat and finds pine tar is more than 18 inches from the knob—a rules violation. McClelland calls Brett out, ending the game to give the Yankees a 4-3 win. Brett goes berserk at the ruling and the Royals protest the game.

July 27 - The Royals' Gaylord Perry records his 3,500th career strikeout; he is the fourth pitcher to attain that mark. The Royals beat Cleveland, 5-4.

July 28 - American League President Lee MacPhail upholds the Royals' protest of the Pine Tar game. MacPhail finds that Brett's bat was not "altered to improve the distance factor." Brett's home run is allowed and MacPhail orders the game resumed from the point of the dispute—two out in the top of the ninth with the Royals ahead 5-4.

August 5 - Waivers are asked on Vida Blue for the purpose of giving him his unconditional release from the Royals.

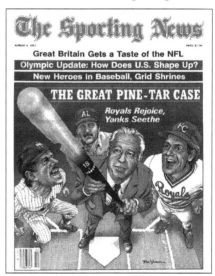

The Pine Tar game made national headlines.

I've never been that mad in my whole life.

George Brett
on the Pine Tar Incident

41

August 18 - Pine Tar game conclusion. 1,245 fans turn out at Yankee Stadium to see Hal McRae strike out and pitcher Dan Quisenberry retire the Yankees in order in the bottom of the 9th inning. The Royals win the much protested game, 5-4.

> *I expected something more exciting. It was an ordinary game except for one thing: I didn't give up a hit.*
>
> **Dan Quisenberry**
> on finishing the Pine Tar game

August 23 - Amos Otis collects his 2,000th career hit, a single, in Kansas City's 10-2 win over Chicago at Royals Stadium.

September 13 - Dan Quisenberry breaks John Hiller's all-time single-season save record, notching his 39th of the season in the Royals' 4-3 win over the Angels.

October 2 - The Royals lose at Oakland, 8-4, ending the season with a 79-83 mark, their worst record since 1974.

Dan Quisenberry

Pine Boxes

Before the Royals protest was upheld and the Pine Tar Game was ordered to be resumed at the point following George Brett's home run, the box dated July 24, 1983, was the official record of the game. After the replay, the box dated August 18, 1983, became the official box for the game. Although not recorded in the box because it wasn't an official figure, the conclusion of the game attracted only 1,245 fans. Yankee manager Billy Martin was responsible for most of the changes in the box score because of his numerous lineup alterations.

July 24, 1983

Kansas City (3)

	AB	R	H	BI
Wilson, cf	3	0	0	0
Sheridan, cf	2	0	0	0
Washington, ss	5	0	1	0
Brett, 3b	5	0	2	0
McRae, dh	3	0	0	0
Otis, rf	4	0	1	0
Wathan, 1b	3	2	1	0
Roberts, lf	3	0	2	0
Aikens, 1b	1	0	0	0
White, 2b	4	1	2	2
Slaught, c	4	0	3	1
Totals	37	3	12	3

New York (4)

	AB	R	H	BI
Campaneris, 2b	4	1	2	0
Nettles, 3b	3	0	0	0
Piniella, rf	4	1	1	0
Mumphrey, cf	0	0	0	0
Baylor, dh	4	1	1	2
Winfield, cf	4	1	3	2
Kemp, lf	4	0	0	0
Balboni, 1b	2	0	0	0
Mattingly, rf	1	0	0	0
Smalley, ss	3	0	1	0
Cerone, c	2	0	0	0
Totals	31	4	8	4

KANSAS CITY	010	101	000—3	
NEW YORK	010	003	00x—4	

DP—New York 1. LOB—KC 9, New York 5.
3B—White, Slaught, Baylor, HR—Winfield (16).
GAME-WINNING RBI—Winfield (13).

	IP	H	R	ER	BB	SO
Kansas City						
Black (L, 4-4)	6	7	4	4	0	2
Armstrong	2	1	0	0	2	0
New York						
Rawley	5-1/3	10	3	3	2	2
D. Murry (W, 3-1)	3-1/3	2	0	0	0	2
Gossage (S, 12)	1/3	0	0	0	0	0

T—2:40. A—33,944.

August 18, 1983

Kansas City (5)

	AB	R	H	BI
Wilson, cf	3	0	0	0
Sheridan, cf	2	0	0	0
Simpson, lf	0	0	0	0
Washington, ss	5	1	1	0
Brett, 3b	5	1	3	2
Pryor, 3b	0	0	0	0
McRae, dh	4	0	0	0
Otis, rf	4	0	1	0
Wathan, 1b	3	2	1	0
Roberts, lf	3	0	2	0
Aikens, 1b	1	0	0	0
White, 2b	4	1	2	2
Slaught, c	4	0	3	1
Totals	38	5	13	5

New York (4)

	AB	R	H	BI
Campaneris, 2b	4	1	2	0
Griffey, 1b	0	0	0	0
Nettles, 3b	3	0	0	0
Piniella, rf	4	1	1	0
Mumphrey, cf	0	0	0	0
Wynegar, c	0	0	0	0
Baylor, dh	4	1	1	2
Winfield, cf	4	1	3	2
Kemp, lf	4	0	0	0
Balboni, 1b	2	0	0	0
Mattingly, rf	2	0	0	0
Smalley, ss	4	0	1	0
Cerone, c	2	0	0	0
Guidry, cf	0	0	0	0
Gamble, ph	1	0	0	0
Totals	34	4	8	4

KANSAS CITY	010	101	002—5	
NEW YORK	010	003	000—4	

DP—New York 1. LOB—KC 8, New York 5.
3B—White, Slaught, Baylor, HR—Winfield (16), Brett (20).
GAME-WINNING RBI—Brett (10).

	IP	H	R	ER	BB	SO
Kansas City						
Black	6	7	4	4	0	2
Armstrong (W, 6-6)	2	1	0	0	2	0
Quisenberry (S,33)	1	0	0	0	0	0
New York						
Rawley	5-1/3	10	3	3	2	2
D. Murry	3-1/3	2	1	1	0	2
Gossage (L, 10-4)	0	1	1	1	0	0
Frazier	1/3	0	0	0	0	1

* Pitched to one batter in the ninth.
T—2:52. A—33,944.

October 14 - Kansas City Royals' players Willie Wilson, Willie Aikens, and Jerry Martin, along with former Royal Vida Blue, plead guilty to one count of conspiring to attempt to possess cocaine.

December 8 - Steve Balboni comes to Kansas City from the Yankees with Roger Erickson in exchange for Mike Armstrong and Duane Dewey.

December 15 - Royals' players Willie Aikens, Willie Wilson, and Jerry Martin, with Vida Blue, are suspended for one year by Commissioner Bowie Kuhn. An arbitrator later shortens the suspensions.

December 19 - Amos Otis, after 14 seasons with the Royals, leaves the team a free agent and signs a one-year contract with the Pirates. The Royals continue their house-cleaning by trading Willie Aikens to Toronto for Jorge Orta.

1984

April 3 - The Royals open the season in New York and beat the Yankees, 4-2. Buddy Black wins for KC.

April 19 - Bret Saberhagen wins his first major league game, beating the Tigers, 5-2.

May 23 - Bud Black pitches a gem as the Royals defeat the White Sox at Royals Stadium, 1-0.

June 25 - Kansas City crushes the A's in Kansas City, 16-0. Gubicza gets the win.

July 1 - Paul Splittorff retires. His 166 wins in 13 seasons are the most in the history of the club.

August 5 - Charlie Leibrandt shuts out the Tigers in Detroit, 4-0.

Bret Saberhagen

September 12 - The Royals beat the Minnesota Twins 3-2 and Dan Quisenberry—saving the game for Bud Black—becomes the first pitcher in major league history to record 40 or more saves in two consecutive seasons.

September 28 - The Royals clinch the American League West, beating the A's in Oakland, 6-5. Charlie Leibrandt is the winning pitcher for the Royals.

September 30 - Oakland beats Kansas City on the last day of the season, 8-2. The Royals finish with a record of 84-78.

October 2 - Game 1 of the ALCS. The Tigers overpower Kansas City at Royals Stadium and win going away, 8-1. Buddy Black is ineffective as the Royals' starter and takes the loss.

> *I never blamed anyone else for what I did. The Royals have done a lot for me, and I don't want them to think about me now. I just want them to have a good season.*
> **Willie Wilson, 1984**

> *I never really thought I would see another playoff in Kansas City. We made so many changes so fast, I had a feeling it was going to be a few years before we came together and could contend.*
> **Frank White**
> after clinching the 1984 AL West

The Royals celebrate after clinching the 1984 AL West Division title.

45

October 3 - Game 2 of the ALCS. Bret Saberhagen is brilliant, but the Royals are unable to score in extra frames and lose 5-3 in 11 innings as Detroit's John Grubb delivers a two-run double. Quiz loses, and KC heads to Detroit down two games to none.

October 5 - Game 3 of the ALCS. Despite throwing a three-hitter, Charlie Leibrandt receives no offensive help and the Royals lose, 1-0, and are swept out of the ALCS by the Tigers.

Don Slaught and Bud Black in the 1984 ALCS.

1985

January 7 - U.L. Washington is traded to the Montreal Expos for two minor leaguers.

January 18 - In a key move, the Royals acquire catcher Jim Sundberg from the Milwaukee Brewers in a four-team deal that sends catcher Don Slaught to Texas and pitcher Frank Wills to the Mets. Sundberg provides needed stability behind the plate throughout the 1985 season.

February 22 - Dan Quisenberry, Willie Wilson and Frank White are offered lifetime contracts.

April 8 - Buddy Black and Quisenberry combine for a five-hitter as the Royals defeat the Blue Jays, 2-1, before an opening day crowd of 41,086.

April 30 - Steve Balboni swats a grand slam and Bret Saberhagen throws a five-hitter as the Royals defeat the Indians 5-1.

May 3 - The Royals turn their first triple play since 1972 but lose to the Yankees, 7-1.

May 17 - A good trade. The Royals acquire Lonnie Smith from the St. Louis Cardinals for outfielder John Morris. Smith becomes the team's leadoff man.

May 18 - Larry Gura is released from the team. His career record with the club stands at 111-78.

June 7 - Steve Balboni hits two home runs in KC's 6-0 win over the Angels.

June 24 - McRae hits two homers, and Motley, Smith, and Sundberg hit one each in the Royals' 12-6 win over the Twins.

July 11 - George Brett is elected the starting third baseman on the American League All-Star team for the 10th straight year.

August 24 - Brett drives in four runs as the Royals defeat the Rangers 8-2.

September 6 - The Royals sweep a doubleheader from the Brewers, 4-3 and 7-1. The wins move the team into first place.

September 10 - Hal McRae collects his 2,000th career hit, an RBI double, in the Royals' 6-0 win over the Angels.

September 20 - Balboni hits a grand slam, leading the Royals to a 5-1 win over the Twins.

September 30 - Saberhagen pitches a five-hitter and earns his 20th win of the season, a 3-1 victory over the Angels that moves the Royals into a tie for first place.

Steve Balboni

Lonnie Smith

October 3 - Jackson defeats the Angels 4-1, giving the Royals a one-game lead. White, Brett and Balboni homer.

October 5 - The Royals clinch their sixth division title in ten years, defeating the A's 5-4. Brett homers for the fifth time in six games and Quisenberry gets the win in relief.

Can you believe we won this thing? Look at our stats.
Dane Iorg
on winning the 1985 AL West

October 6 - Kansas City closes the regular season losing to the A's, 9-3. The team finishes with a record of 91-71.

October 8 - Game 1 of the ALCS. Dave Stieb shuts down the Royals as the Blue Jays win in Toronto, 6-1. Leibrandt is the losing pitcher for Kansas City.

October 9 - Game 2 of the ALCS. The Royals lose, 6-5.

Danny Jackson

October 11 - Game 3 of the ALCS. Brett homers twice to lead the Royals to a 6-5 come-from-behind win. Steve Farr pitches 4-and-a-third innings of shutout relief.

October 12 - Game 4 of the ALCS. The Royals fall behind three games to one, losing 3-1.

October 13 - Game 5 of the ALCS. Danny Jackson tosses a shutout at the Blue Jays, allowing only eight hits to win 2-0. The Royals head back to Toronto down three games to two.

October 15 - Game 6 of the ALCS. Brett ties the ALCS with another home run off Alexander as the Royals win 5-3. The series is now tied at three games apiece.

Charlie Leibrandt

Hal McRae congratulates George Brett after one of his two home runs in Game 3 of the 1985 ALCS.

The Royals celebrate after defeating Toronto to win the 1985 American League pennant.

October 16 - Game 7 of the ALCS. Back to the World Series! The Royals complete their improbable comeback by defeating Toronto 6-2 in Game 7 of the ALCS and win the American League pennant. Jim Sundberg provides the big blow, a bases-loaded triple in the sixth inning. The Cardinals await Kansas City in the World Series.

We're not a dominant club, but we played about as well as you can the last six weeks of the season. We earned this thing.

Dick Howser
on the 1985 Royals

October 19 - World Series Game 1. Cardinal Pitcher John Tudor controls the Royals and with relief help from Todd Worrell, wins 3-1 at Royals Stadium. Danny Jackson is the losing pitcher.

October 20 - World Series Game 2. Late-inning heartbreak for Charlie Leibrandt. After limiting the Cardinals to just 2 hits through 8 innings, Charlie gives up 4 runs and loses the game. It is the first time since the 1939 World Series a team will come back from 2-0 deficit in the 9th inning to win. The teams head to St. Louis with the Cardinals up, two games to none.

Frank White circles the bases after slugging a two-run home run in Game 3 of the 1985 World Series. The shot led the way to the Royals' 6-1 win.

George Brett tags out the Cardinals' Willie McGee.

October 22 - World Series Game 3. Bret Saberhagen limits the Redbirds to six singles and Frank White provides the needed offensive punch with a homer and three RBIs. The Royals win the game, 6-1.

October 23 - World Series Game 4. John Tudor is again masterful, limiting Kansas City to 5 hits and shutting them out, 3-0. The win gives the Cardinals a 3-1 advantage in the series. Although he pitches well, Buddy Black takes the loss.

October 24 - World Series Game 5. Danny Jackson pitches brilliantly and stops St. Louis. The Royals win 6-1 to send the series back to Kansas City.

> *Everything we do not only surprises me but everybody else.*
> **George Brett**
> on Game 6 of 1985 World Series

> *No one in the park was sober.*
> *The sudden emotional surge, from severe communal depression to sudden shared ecstasy, was as intoxicating as rum...People jumped up and down until the stadium shook. Strange men hugged each other and wept with joy...A continuous roar sailed through the air for nearly twenty minutes, until every pair of lungs in the county was too hoarse to contribute any more to it.*
> **Bill James**
> ***The 1986 Bill James Baseball Abstract***
> on the Royals winning Game 6 of the 1985 World Series

Jim Sundberg slides across home plate with the winning run in Game 6 of the 1985 World Series. The Royals' Lonnie Smith looks on as St. Louis catcher Darrell Porter misses the tag.

October 26 - World Series Game 6. The Royals use a controversial call at first base, a couple of Cardinal miscues and solid clutch hitting to rally in the bottom of the 9th inning and win, 2-1, sending the series to a seventh game. Dane Iorg, batting for Dan Quisenberry, lines a two-run single to right field to send the Royals home winners and forever put a stamp of what-might-have-been on this game for the Cardinals. Quiz gets the win.

October 27 - World Series Game 7. **THE ROYALS WIN THE WORLD SERIES!** Bret Saberhagen glides through the St. Louis hitters the entire game, while the Royals explode for 11 runs. After Darryl Motley hits a two-run homer in the second inning, it's easy cruising for the Royals, who collect 14 hits in the game. Saberhagen wins the World Series MVP.

November 18 - Bret Saberhagen wins the American League Cy Young Award.

> *There were times when I thought it would take a miracle for us to win this year, but we never gave up. This is incredible.*
>
> **Jim Sundberg**
> after Game 7 of World Series

World champions! Steve Balboni, George Brett, Bret Saberhagen and Jim Sundberg celebrate following the final out of the 1985 World Series.

The 1985 World Champion Kansas City Royals.

1986

April 1 - Kansas City obtains Angel Salazar from the Mets for Tony Ferreira. Salazar will be the Royals' Opening Day shortstop.

April 8 - The Royals drop the season opener to the Yankees in New York, 4-3. Buddy Black is the losing pitcher.

April 12 - Pitcher Dennis Leonard pitches a three-hit shutout against Toronto after three years of inactivity due to four different surgeries.

May 25 - George Brett collects his 2,000th career hit in Kansas City's 2-1 win over the White Sox.

June 7 - The Royals pick Bo Jackson in the 4th round of the June draft.

June 8 - David Cone makes his major league debut with the Royals, giving up three hits and one run in one inning of work.

June 10 - Brett rips five hits against the Mariners at Royals Stadium. Kansas City wins, 9-5.

June 21 - Bo Jackson signs with the Royals.

The Royals are presented the 1985 World Series trophy at the team's 1986 home opener.

June 30 - Bo Jackson makes his professional debut with the Memphis Chicks.

July 8 - The Royals lose to Baltimore in 13 innings at Royals Stadium, 8-4. It's the team's 11th straight loss, a club record.

July 9 - Danny Jackson shuts out the Orioles, 3-0, to end the 11-game losing streak.

July 15 - Dick Howser manages the American League All Star team to a 3-2 win in Houston. Frank White homers for the AL.

July 18 - The Royals announce Howser will miss the rest of the season to undergo treatment for a brain tumor that is later revealed to be malignant. Third base coach Mike Ferraro takes over the managing duties for the rest of the season.

> *Losing Dick (Howser) was an absolute shock....It put some fear in us. You had to wonder if baseball was really that important.*
> **Jamie Quirk, 1986**

September 14 - Bo Jackson hits his first major-league home run, a 475-foot blast off Seattle's Mike Moore in a 10-3 win at Royals Stadium.

October 5 - The Royals end the season losing to the A's in Oakland, 6-0. Saberhagen takes the loss as Kansas City finishes with a record of 76-86.

December 10 - The Royals acquire Danny Tartabull and Rick Luecken from the Mariners for Mike Kingery, Scott Bankhead and Steve Shields.

1987

February 23 - Lacking the strength to work, Dick Howser steps down in his bid to return as the Royals' manager. Billy Gardner is named as his replacement.

March 27 - The Royals trade David Cone and Chris Jelic to the Mets for Ed Hearn, Rick Anderson and Mauro Gozzo.

April 6 - The Royals lose to the White Sox on Opening Day at Royals Stadium, 5-4. Danny Jackson suffers the loss.

May 13 - Willie Wilson collects five hits as the Royals win at Baltimore in 12 innings, 8-7.

June 17 - Dick Howser dies at St. Luke's Hospital in Kansas City.

July 3 - The Royals retire Howser's uniform number, 10.

Danny Tartabull

July 14 - Bo Jackson announces that he will play football for the Los Angeles Raiders as a "hobby."

August 2 - Royals' rookie Kevin Seitzer goes 6-for-6 with two home runs and seven RBIs, tying the AL record for hits in a nine-inning game. Kansas City handily beats the Red Sox, 13-5.

August 27 - Billy Gardner is fired. John Wathan is named to manage the Royals. The Royals beat Texas, 3-2, on Brett's 10th-inning home run.

> *It was the worst (atmosphere) since I've been playing. I couldn't wait till the season ended.*
>
> **Frank White**
> on the 1987 season

October 4 - The Royals clobber Minnesota in the season finale at home, 10-1. Gubicza gets the win as the Royals finish with a record of 83-79, second in the AL West.

> *The whole traumatic thing about this year was that we could have won it; we could have won the whole thing.*
> **Frank White, 1987**

November 6 - Kansas City sends Danny Jackson and Angel Salazar to the Reds for Kurt Stillwell and Ted Power.

1988

February 2 - The Royals obtain Jeff Montgomery from the Reds for Van Snider.

April 4 - Saberhagen gives up three home runs to Toronto's George Bell and the Royals lose the season opener, 5-3, at Royals Stadium.

June 3 - Kansas City trades Buddy Black to the Indians for Pat Tabler.

June 16 - The Royals beat the A's at Oakland, 9-5. It's the team's 13th win in 14 games and pulls them to within 4 1/2 games of first place. Gubizca gets the win.

Kevin Seitzer

July 4 - The Royals release Dan Quisenberry.

September 20 - Danny Tartabull hits his third grand slam of the season, but the Royals still lose to the Mariners in Seattle, 11-10.

September 26 - Mark Gubicza blanks Seattle at Royals Stadium, 5-0, to win his 20th game of the season.

October 2 - Chicago beats the Royals, 5-1, in the last game of the season. Kansas City finishes with a record of 84-77, third in the AL West.

November 30 - The Royals sign free-agent catcher Bob Boone.

1989

April 3 - Kansas City drops the season opener to Toronto at Royals Stadium, 4-3. Mark Gubicza is the losing pitcher.

July 11 - Bo Jackson is voted the Most Valuable Player in the All Star Game at Anaheim. Jackson homers and steals a base as the American League wins, 5-3.

> *In a lot of ways it was a good year. But for a team which was thinking pennant from day one, it wasn't good enough.*
>
> **John Wathan**
> **on the 1989 season**

August 24 - The Royals lose to California, 5-0, ending the team's nine-game winning streak.

September 8 - Brett singles for his 2,500th career hit as the Royals beat the Twins, 6-0.

September 28 - The Royals are shut out for the 18th time this season, losing at California, 2-0.

October 1 - Oakland beats the Royals 4-3 in the season's final game. Kansas City finishes with a mark of 92-70, good for second place in the AL West.

November 15 - Bret Saberhagen wins the American League Cy Young Award for the second time. Saberhagen received 27 of 28 possible first place votes for his 23-6, 2.16 ERA season.

December 12 - Mark Davis signs a four-year multi-million dollar contract with the Royals. The star relief pitcher won the National League Cy Young Award in 1989, making the Royals the first team ever to have both defending winners on the same team.

December 15 - Goodbye Charlie. The Royals trade Charlie Leibrandt and Rick Luecken to the Braves for Gerald Perry and Jim LeMasters.

Bo Jackson

1990

March 31 - The Royals trade Jose DeJesus to the Phillies for Steve Jeltz.

April 9 - The Royals lose to Baltimore in 11 innings at Royals Stadium, 7-6, to start the season. Jeff Montgomery is pinned with the defeat.

April 14 - The Royals beat Toronto, 3-1, with Saberhagen getting the win and Mark Davis the save. It is the first time ever that two reigning Cy Young Award winners have figured in the same victory.

June 13 - Willie Wilson steals his 600th career base in the Royals' 11-4 win over the Angels.

July 17 - Great news, bad news. Bo Jackson homers three times at Yankee Stadium off Andy Hawkins, but suffers minor tissue damage to his shoulder diving for a ball in the outfield. The injury causes him to miss more than a month of playing time.

Willie Wilson

July 25 - For the second time in his career, George Brett hits for the cycle. The Royals defeat Toronto, 6-1.

August 26 - In his first game after six weeks on the DL, Bo Jackson homers in his first at bat to tie a major league record with four consecutive homers. KC wins at home over Seattle, 8-2.

October 3 - Brett wins his third batting title, finishing the season with a batting average of .329. He is the first player in major league history to win three batting titles in three different decades. The Royals still lose at Cleveland in the season's last game, 5-2. The team's final record is 75-86.

> *We just screwed it up from the beginning (of the season). From beginning to end.*
>
> **Bo Jackson**
> on the 1990 season

October 10 - Herk Robinson is named as the Royals new General Manager.

November 21 - KC signs free-agent pitcher Mike Boddicker to a three-year contract.

December 1 - The Royals sign free-agent outfielder/DH Kirk Gibson.

1991

January - Ewing Kauffman buys back Avron Fogelman's 49 percent of the team, and is again the sole owner of the club.

March 15 - The Royals release Bo Jackson. After injuring his hip while playing football, it appears his career is over. The Royals pay off a termination fee for his contract. When placed on waivers, all major league teams pass on Jackson.

April 8 - The Royals win on Opening Day, beating the Indians at Royals Stadium, 4-2. Saberhagen is the winning pitcher.

May 22 - John Wathan is fired. Hal McRae replaces him as the Royals' manager.

Kirk Gibson

May 24 - McRae loses his managerial debut, 3-2, at Minnesota.

June 6 - The Royals win the longest game in team history, 4-3 in 18 innings against the Rangers at Royals Stadium. Mike Boddicker gets the win after 6 hours and 28 minutes.

July 6 - Danny Tartabull hits three homers against the A's, the only Royals' player to do so at Royals Stadium. The A's still win, 9-7.

July 17 - The Royals win another long game, this time 15 innings, dropping Baltimore at home, 9-8.

August 26 - Bret Saberhagen throws a no-hitter against Chicago at Royals Stadium, striking out five and walking two in the 7-0 win.

Bret Saberhagen

This is something I'll remember forever. But truthfully, you have to give credit to everyone behind me. And you have to have some luck to do this.
Bret Saberhagen, 1991
after his no-hitter

October 6 - Kansas City loses the last game of the season at California, 3-1. Mark Davis is the loser. The team finishes with a record of 82-80.

December 9 - The Royals sign free-agent first baseman Wally Joyner.

December 11 - Bombshell trade. Kansas City parts with Bret Saberhagen, sending him and Bill Pecota to the Mets for Gregg Jefferies, Keith Miller and Kevin McReynolds. In other deals, the team also unloads Storm Davis and Todd Benzinger.

1992

January 6 - Danny Tartabull leaves the Royals, signing a contract with the Yankees.

March 10 - The Royals trade Kirk Gibson to the Pirates for Neal Heaton.

April 6 - Kansas City drops the season opener at Oakland, 5-3.

July 21 - Free agent disappointment. After 2 1/2 years of poor performances, the Royals unload Mark Davis to the Braves for Juan Berenguer.

August 29 - Kansas City sends Sean Berry and Archie Corbin to the Expos for Chris Haney and Bill Sampen.

> *It happened so quick, I really didn't have time to prepare myself for it... But I'm relieved, very relieved.*
>
> **George Brett, 1992**
> after getting his 3,000th hit

September 30 - 3,000 hits! George Brett goes 4-for-4 at Anaheim, giving him 3,000 major-league hits for his career. The 3,000th hit is off the Angels' Julio Valero. The Royals win, 4-0.

October 4 - The Royals lose at home to Minnesota in the last game of the year, 6-0. The team finishes at 72-90, their worst record since 1970.

November 19 - The Royals trade Dennis Moeller and Joel Johnston to the Pirates for second baseman Jose Lind.

December 8 - The Royals sign free-agent David Cone to a three-year, $18 million contract, making him the game's highest-paid pitcher. The Royals also sign free-agent shortstop Greg Gagne.

1993

February 12 - Gregg Jefferies and Ed Gerald are sent to St. Louis for Felix Jose and Craig Wilson.

April 5 - The Red Sox spoil the home opener for the Royals, winning 3-1. Roger Clemens is the winner for Boston, Appier takes the loss for KC.

May 13 - Brett hits the 300th home run of his career at Cleveland Stadium off the Indians' Mark Clark. The Royals win the game, 7-3.

June 19 - Kansas City signs free-agent third baseman Gary Gaetti.

Greg Gagne

July 2 - Royals Stadium is officially renamed Kauffman Stadium.

August 1 - Royals owner Ewing Kauffman dies at the age of 76.

> *The game became a job. It wasn't a game anymore. And baseball shouldn't be treated that way.*
> **George Brett, 1993**

September 29 - Brett singles in his final at bat at Kauffman Stadium. Kansas City beats Cleveland, 3-2.

October 3 - The Royals finish the season at Texas and win, 4-1. It is also Brett's final game as a Royal. Jeff Montgomery posts his 45th save, tops in the AL, as well as tying Dan Quisenberry for the all-time Royals' mark. Finally, Kevin Appier becomes the second Royal ever to win the AL's ERA crown, finishing with a 2.56 mark. The team finishes with an 84-78 mark, finishing third in the AL West.

1994

January 5 - Kevin McReynolds is unloaded on the Mets for Vince Coleman.

April 4 - The Royals open the season at Baltimore and lose, 6-3. Appier is the losing pitcher for KC.

May 14 - George Brett's number 5 is retired and he is inducted into the Royals Hall of Fame.

July 16 - Wally Joyner collects five hits against the Tigers at Kauffman Stadium, but the Royals still lose, 13-7.

Wally Joyner

July 23 - David Cone beats the Tigers in Detroit, 4-1. It is the first win in what will become a 14-game winning streak.

August 6 - The streak is over. The Royals' 14-game winning streak is halted by the Seattle Mariners in a game moved to Kauffman Stadium, on short notice, due to structural damage at the Kingdome. Seattle wins big, 11-2, as Gubicza takes the loss.

> *I try to put myself in the shoes of the fans. I come up with the same question, 'What are we going to give back to the fan?'*
> **David Cone, 1994**
> **on the players' strike**

August 10 - The Royals lose at California, 2-1, and the baseball season ends the next day because of the players' strike.

September 14 - The rest of the 1994 season, including the World Series, is officially canceled.

October 7 - Hal McRae is fired as the Royals' manager and replaced by Bob Boone.

October 22 - Bob Hamelin wins the American League Rookie of the Year Award.

October 25 - David Cone becomes the second Royals' pitcher to win the American League Cy Young Award.

Bob Hamelin

Winter - The artificial turf at Kauffman Stadium is replaced with grass. Also, the fences from left center field to right center field are moved in 10 feet.

1995

March 17 - Muriel Kauffman passes away.

April 5 - Brian McRae is traded to the Cubs for Derek Wallace and Geno Morones.

April 6 - For the second time in his career, David Cone is traded from the Royals. This time KC sends him to Toronto for Chris Stynes, David Sinnes and Tony Medrano.

April 26 - Opening Day. Kauffman Stadium has a grass field for the first time. The Royals beat the Orioles, 5-1, with Appier getting the win.

David Cone

April 29 - Jon Nunnally leads off the game against the Yankees with a home run, becoming the 70th player—and first member of the Royals—to homer in his first major league at bat. The Royals lose 10-3 at Kauffman Stadium.

June 16 - The Royals extend their win-streak to seven games with a 3-1, 13-inning win over Oakland. Jeff Montgomery pitches a perfect 13th inning to pick up the save.

June 21 - Montgomery notches his 200th career save against the Angels in California. The Royals win, 6-3.

> *I love the four-day rotation. The more I can pitch, the better.*
>
> **Kevin Appier, 1995**

July 2 - The Royals retire Frank White's No. 20 and induct him into the Royals Hall of Fame. KC loses to the White Sox, 6-5, in 10 innings.

July 30 - The Royals wear replicas of the 1924 Kansas City Monarchs uniforms during their game with the Tigers at Kauffman Stadium. The Tigers wear 1920 Detroit Stars uniforms as the two team commemorate Negro League baseball. Kansas City wins, 3-2, and Montgomery gets the save.

August 15 - The Royals trade Vince Coleman to Seattle for a player to be named later.

September 1 - The Royals defeat the Rangers, 5-2, for their sixth win in a row. It is also the team's eighth win in their last nine games and gives them a lead in the American League wild card race. Gordon gets the win against Texas.

> *We've got to get our act together. We have to have a gut-check and know what's in front of us. We've played well all year and then, right by the All-Star break, we couldn't find ourselves.*
>
> **Tom Gordon, 1995**

September 23 - Kansas City loses their 6th game in a row to Cleveland, 7-3. The loss virtually eliminates the team from the AL wild card race. Tom Gordon takes the loss.

October 1 - The Royals get hammered by Cleveland in the last game of the year, 17-7. They finish with a mark of 70-74, which is surprisingly good enough for 2nd place in the AL Central.

December 9 - After spending the 1995 season with the Red Sox, catcher Mike MacFarlane returns to KC, signing as a free agent with the Royals.

December 17 - Jose Offerman comes to the Royals from Los Angeles in exchange for pitcher Billy Brewer.

December 21 - The Royals trade Wally Joyner to San Diego for infielder-outfielder Bip Roberts. Tom Gordon leaves Kansas City, opting to sign a three-year deal with the Red Sox.

> *We didn't mean to play it that way. We have had a lot of trouble scoring points.*
>
> **Bob Boone, 1995**
> after getting swept by the A's

Winter - Gary Gaetti leaves the Royals, signing with St. Louis. Greg Gagne also opts for free agency and inks a deal with the Los Angeles Dodgers.

1996

February 17 - The Royals sign free-agent pitcher Tim Belcher to a one-year contract.

April 2 - Kansas City loses the season opener in Baltimore, 4-2. Appier takes the loss.

April 3 - Kansas City turns a triple play on the Orioles but still lose, 7-1. Gubicza is KC's losing pitcher.

April 13 - Despite getting only one hit, Kansas City beats the Brewers in Milwaukee, 3-2. Michael Tucker follows a pair of walks with a three-run homer for the game winner. Gubicza gets the win.

May 12 - The Royals steal six bases against the Mariners but lose anyway, 8-5.

May 24 - Mark Gubicza wins his last game as a Royal, pitching a complete-game shutout against the Rangers at Kauffman Stadium, 8-0.

> *He already is going to punch me in the mouth if he doesn't pitch on Saturday.*
>
> **Bob Boone, 1996**
> joking about Appier's reaction if he has to miss a start

June 1 - Jeff Montgomery makes his 500th appearance for the Royals. He also takes the loss for the game as Kansas City loses to the Blue Jays, 5-3 in 10 innings.

July 20 - Jeff Montgomery saves the 239th game of his career to pass Dan Quisenberry and set a new Royals' team record. Kansas City defeats the White Sox in Chicago, 7-5.

August 10 - Johnny Damon belts a grand slam off California's Jim Abbott. The Royals pound the Angels, 18-3.

August 24 - As they did the year before, the Royals and Tigers wear the uniforms of the Detroit Stars and Kansas City Monarchs. The Royals win the game, 9-2.

September 29 - The Royals end the season with a win over Cleveland at home, 4-1. Belcher earns his 15th win of the season. Kansas City finishes with a 75-86 record, and is the first Royals team in the club's history to end the season in last place.

Jeff Montgomery

October 28 - After 13 seasons in Royal blue, Mark Gubicza is traded to the Angels for DH Chili Davis.

December 13 - Kansas City acquires Jay Bell and Jeff King from Pittsburgh in exchange for Joe Randa, Jeff Granger, Jeff Wallace and Jeff Martin.

1997

January 28 - Kansas City acquires Yamil Benitez from the Expos for Melvin Bunch.

March 26 - The Royals place DH/1B Bob Hamelin, the 1994 American League Rookie of the year, on waivers for the purpose of giving him his unconditional release.

April 2 - Kansas City drops the season opener in Baltimore, 4-2. Jamie Walker takes the loss in relief.

April 7 - The numbers of George Brett (5), the late Dick Howser (10) and Frank White (20) are officially retired before the game and permanently displayed at the bottom of the Kauffman Stadium scoreboard. The Royals add to the festivities by winning their home opener over the Orioles, 6-5.

June 7 - Chili Davis homers from both sides of the plate against Texas at Kauffman Stadium, the 10th time in his 16-year career the veteran DH has accomplished the feat. He is the third Royal to turn the trick.

If he can't find me a reliever, then I can't win.

Bob Boone, 1997
on Royals GM Herk Robinson

June 13 - The Royals play in their first inter-league game at Pittsburgh, losing to the Pirates, 5-3.

July 8 - Bob Boone is fired as the Royals' manager. Tony Muser is named the club's new manager.

July 10 - Kansas City drops Muser's managerial debut to the White Sox at home, 6-3.

July 12 - The Royals honor Jackie Robinson in pregame ceremonies and unveil a permanent display of his signature and, along with all of Major League Baseball, retire his jersey number 42 at the base of the Jumbotron screen behind left field. Royals' outfielder Tom Goodwin will be allowed to continue wearing number 42.

Kevin Appier

July 13 - The Royals lose for the 12th straight time, a new club record. The White Sox outlast KC at Kauffman Stadium, 7-6.

July 25 - Kansas City trades outfielder Tom Goodwin to the Texas Rangers for third baseman Dean Palmer.

August 12 - Jeff Montgomery becomes the 12th major leaguer to accumulate 250 career saves. The Royals beat the Yankees in New York, 6-4.

August 29 - The Royals and Cardinals play for the first time since the 1985 World Series. The Cardinals win at Kauffman Stadium, 9-7.

Mike MacFarlane

August 30 - Five different Royals hit home runs as Kansas City clobbers the Cardinals in the second game of their inter-league series, 16-5. A brawl erupts in the fourth inning after St. Louis pitcher Mark Petkovsek hits Kansas City's Johnny Damon with a pitch and Damon charges the mound. Petkovsek had just given up a grand slam to Jermaine Dye, giving the Royals a 14-1 lead. Both benches and bullpens empty onto the field.

August 31 - Bip Roberts is traded to the Cleveland Indians for right-handed minor league pitcher Roland de la Maza.

Jeff King

September 27 - The Royals finish the season with a win at Chicago, beating the White Sox 10-4. Bones gets the win as Kansas City finishes in last place in the AL Central for the second straight year with a record of 67-93.

It's been my dream for about 30 years to have an opportunity to take a team and make it better. I'd had eight interviews. But it was like I'd had eight at-bats and never hit the ball out of the infield. I hope I spend the rest of my baseball career in Kansas City.

Tony Muser, 1997

September 30 - Royals first baseman Jeff King is tabbed American League Player of the Week. King hit four home runs and knocked in 14 runs in the final week of the season.

November 1 - After weeks of speculation about a possible move to the National League as part of Major League Baseball's realignment process, it is announced that the Royals will remain in the American League, staying in the Central Division.

November 20 - Jeff Conine, taken by the Florida Marlins when the Royals   him unprotected in the 1992 expansion draft, is traded back to KC for minor-league pitcher Blaine Mull.

Johnny Damon

December 22 - The Royals sign free-agent Hal Morris.

1998

January 20 -The Royals sign veteran infielder Terry Pendleton and Lee Smith, all-time leader in saves, to minor league contracts. Pendleton makes the club, but Smith retires when he is asked to start the season at Omaha.

March 31 — Kansas City opens the season in Baltimore and wins, 4-1. Tim Belcher pitches well and gets the win. Jeff Montgomery picks up the save.

April 7 - Baltimore spoils the home opener, easily beating the Royals at Kauffman Stadium, 11-7. Glendon Rusch takes the loss.

April 8 -The Royals send catcher Mike MacFarlane to Oakland for outfielder Shane Mack.

May 23 -The Royals lose to the Rangers in Texas, 7-3, the team's eighth straight loss. Glendon Rusch is the loser for Kansas City.

Dean Palmer

June 2 - In the process of losing to the Angels at Kauffman Stadium, six Royals are ejected as the result of an out-of-control beanball war: Manager Tony Muser, Jim Pittsley, coach Rich Dauer, coach Jamie Quirk, Scott Service, and for taking a cheap shot at Angels' Frank Bolick in the ninth inning brawl, Felix Martinez, who wasn't in the lineup. The Angels also suffer six ejections, but they prevail in the game, 7-5. Chris Haney is the losing pitcher for KC.

June 3 - Rookie shortstop Felix Martinez is sent to Omaha.

June 30 -The Royals defeat the Cardinals in St. Louis, 6-1. Cardinal Mark McGwire slams one of his record 70 home runs in the game, but the Royals don't give up anything else. Glendon Rusch picks up the win for Kansas City.

> *I've got to serve my time. It's going to have to be done. I'll take my medicine like a man and do it.*
> **Tony Muser, 1998**
> on serving his
> eight-game suspension

Tony Muser

August 1 - The Royals steal a team record eight bases against the Orioles at Kauffman Stadium and win, 9-5. Jose Offerman leads the way with four steals.

August 20 -The Royals Board of Directors announce that New York attorney Miles Prentice and his group have the best bid to purchase the franchise, but that they are also lacking the required amount of local owners.

> *I got an opportunity to run and we just did it. It's part of our game. Today was a good day for us.*
> **Jose Offerman, 1998**
> on the Royals eight stolen base
> against the Orioles

September 24 - Jeff Montgomery notches his 36th save of the season as the Royals win, 6-4. Jose Rosado gets the club's final win of the year against the White Sox at Kauffman Stadium.

September 27 - Kansas City closes the season with a 7-6 loss to the White Sox. Tim Belcher is the loser for the Royals. The team finishes the season with a 72-89 record and third place finish in the AL Central.

> *I think we'll get it done. I love baseball. I'm still having fun. This has been an interesting odyssey.*
>
> **Miles Prentice, 1998**
> **on buying the Royals**

September 30 - Dan Quisenberry loses his battle with brain cancer and passes away at his home. He was 45 years old.

November 4 - The Royals announce that radio broadcaster Fred White will not return for the 1999 season. White has been a part of the Royals broadcast team for 25 years.

November 13 - Miles Prentice and his group are formally selected by the Royals Board of Directors as the successful bidder for purchasing the Royals. Prominent members of the Prentice Group include Crosby Kemper, Buck O'Neil, Tom Watson, James B. Nutter, Jr., and Nancy Kauffman, Ewing and Muriel's daughter-in-law.

Tim Belcher

December 7 - Jeff Montgomery, the Royals' career saves leader, agrees to a one-year contract worth 2.5 million dollars.

December 10 - Kansas City sends former first-round pick Juan LeBron to the Mets for third baseman and former Royal Joe Randa. The club also signs free-agent shortstop Rey Sanchez.

December 14 -The Royals sign free-agent catcher Chad Kreuter, formerly with the Angels, to a one-year contract.

December 21 - Free-agent pitcher Alvin Morman, formerly with the Giants, signs a one-year contract with the Royals.

1999

January 5 - George Brett is selected for induction into the National Baseball Hall of Fame in Cooperstown, New York. Nolan Ryan and Robin Yount will join Brett in the Hall of Fame.

January 14 - Kansas City re-signs pitcher Scott Service to a one-year contract.

March 30 – The Royals trade cash and a player to be named later to the A's for Jay Witasick. Oakland receives Scott Chiasson on June 10 to complete the deal.

April 2 – The Royals trade Jeff Conine to the Baltimore for Chris Fussell.

April 5 – The Royals open the season with a loss to the Red Sox at Kauffman Stadium. Kevin Appier takes the loss.

May 14 – Mike Sweeney hits a grand slam in Seattle as the Royals win, 12-7.

June 2 – The Royals select three players in the first round of the Amateur Free-agent draft: Kyle Snyder with the seventh overall pick); Mike MacDougal with the 25th overall pick; and Jimmy Gobble with the 43rd overall pick.

June 9 – The Royals win a slugfest against the Cardinals, 17-13, as Joe Randa collects five hits for KC.

July 9 – Joe Randa raps out five hits again, this time against the Astros. The Royals lose, 6-5.

July 25 – George Brett is inducted into the National Baseball Hall of Fame in Cooperstown, New York.

> *My teammates over the last 20 years that I've had, thank you for all your friendship, that's been so important to me. You all have made such an impact on my life. But not only as a player, but as a man. There is one that stands out (points). Jamie Quirk. Thanks.*
>
> **George Brett**
> **during his Hall-of-Fame**
> **induction speech**

> *Hal McRae, whom I consider the best hitting coach in baseball right now. He's the one that taught me how to play the game of baseball. He led by example. He ran balls out, he slid into second, tried to break up double plays. He stretched singles to doubles, doubles to triples. He would do whatever it took to win a ballgame.*
>
> **George Brett**
> **during his Hall-of-Fame**
> **induction speech**

74

July 31 – Kevin Appier is traded to the Oakland Athletics for Jeff D'Amico, Brad Rigby and Blake Stein.

August 25 - Number 300. Jeff Montgomery notches the 300th save of his career as the Royals defeat the Orioles at Kauffman Stadium, 8-6.

September 13 – Tony Muser is ejected for the third time of the season for mocking the umpire. The Royals lose to the Rangers, 8-4.

September 14 – Mark Quinn becomes the third player in MLB history to hit two homers in his major league debut. The Royals lose to the Angles in the second game of a doubleheader, 6-5.

October 2 – The season ends with a 4-3 loss to the Tigers at Kauffman Stadium. The Royals finish with a 64-97 record.

November 9 - Carlos Beltran, the Royals centerfielder is a near-unanimous choice as American League Rookie of the Year. He is the third Royals' player to win the award.

> *I think we can compete for a play-off spot with this team. We have enough talent to do it right now.*
> **George Brett**
> before the start of the 2000 season

November 10 – Royals' pitcher Jeff Montgomery is granted free agency. The Royals All-Time saves leader does pitch again in MLB.

2000

February 18 – The Royals trade Jeremy Giambi to Oakland Athletics for Brett Laxton.

March 14 - Major League Baseball announces the approval of the Glass Family as the new owners of the Royals.

> *I've been told 'You've got to win.' And I'm going to try to.*
> **Tony Muser**
> before the start of the 2000 season

April 9 - The Twins rock the Royals by slamming six home runs at Kauffman Stadium to win easily, 13-7.

April 10 – The Royals walk off with a win thanks to Johnny Damon's home run. KC beats the Twins, 6-5.

April 12 – For the third game in a row, the Royals win with a walk-off home run. This time it's from Rey Sanchez as the Royals defeat Baltimore, 7-6.

April 18 – David Glass becomes the sole owner of the Royals, purchasing the team for $96 million. The Board accepted his offer over a competing bid of $120 million by Miles Prentice.

April 26 – Jermaine Dye hits a grand slam against Tampa Bay as the Royals win, 7-6.

May 26 - The Royals set a team record with four sixth-inning home runs against the Angels in California. Jermaine Dye, Mark Quinn, Brian Johnson, and Carlos Febles all go deep as KC scores eight runs in the inning. KC wins, 9-4.

May 27 – Dave McCarty hits a two-run, pinch-hit home run in the 9th inning to tie the score at Anaheim. The Royals win the game in the 10th, 6-5.

June 17 - Allard Baird replaces Herk Robinson as the new GM of the Royals.

June 29 – Carlos Beltran hits a homer from both sides of the plate to lead the Royals to a 6-1 win over the Indians at Kauffman Stadium.

July 18 – Johnny Damon collects five hits against the Chicago Cubs as the Royals win, 12-4.

July 27 - The Royals release Jamie Walker.

September 1 – Jermaine Dye hits a grand slam at Tampa Bay as Kansas City defeats the Devil Rays, 9-5.

September 15 – Johnny Damon hits a grand slam at Texas, but the Royals lose in 10 innings, 12-11.

October 1 – The Royals defeat the White Sox in Chicago, 6-2, and finish the season with a record of 77-85, good for fourth place in the AL Central.

November 6 - The Royals' right fielder Jermaine Dye wins an American League Gold Glove.

December 18 – The Royals sign Jon Nunnally.

2001

January 18 – Goodbye Johnny. In a three-team trade, the Royals send Johnny Damon and Mark Ellis to Oakland Athletics for Angel Berroa and A.J. Hinch, and also get Roberto Hernandez from Tampa Bay. The Devil Rays send Cory Lidle to Oakland, and the A's send Ben Grieve to Tampa Bay.

> *Chewing on cookies and drinking milk and praying is not going to get it done. It's going to take a lot of hard work and it's a mindset. I'd like to get them to go out and pound tequila (rather) than have cookies and milk because nobody is going to get us out of this but us.*
>
> **Tony Muser**
> during the 2001 season

January 19 – The Royals sign free-agent pitcher Jason Grimsley.

January 22 – The Royals sign free-agent outfielder Raul Ibanez.

April 2 - The Royals drop the season opener to the Yankees in New York, 7-3.

> *I assumed we would walk more and strike out less. I was wrong.*
>
> **Tony Muser**
> at the end of the 2001 season

April 8 - Mark Quinn knocks in five runs as the Royals clobber the Twins at Kauffman Stadium, 15-4.

April 12 - The Royals' game with the Blue Jays at the SkyDome in Toronto is postponed when pieces of the roof fall on the field during batting practice.

May 16 - Joe Randa hits a grand slam as the Royals defeat Tampa Bay, 9-5, at Kauffman Stadium.

June 5 - Kansas City sends Jose Santiago to the Philadelphia Phillies in exchange for pitcher Paul Byrd.

July 14 - Carlos Beltran hits a homer and knocks in four runs as KC defeats the Pirates in Pittsburgh, 7-4, to end a nine-game losing streak.

Carlos Beltran

July 25 - In what could be the worst trade in the history of the franchise, the Royals send outfielder Jermaine Dye to Oakland. In return, the A's trade Mario Encarnacion, Jose Ortiz, and a pitcher to the Rockies, who send Neifi Perez to Kansas City.

August 10 - The beginning of a brawl. Detroit pitcher Doug Weaver refuses to move the resin bag from the front of the pitching mound and then swears at batter Mike Sweeney. The Royals slugger throws his helmet at Weaver, charges the mound, and slams the insolent pitcher to the ground. The two teams then brawled—Sweeney, Royals' pitching coach Al Nipper, and Tigers bench coach Doug Mansolino were ejected. Sweeney received a 10-game suspension. In the end, the Royals win the game, 7-3.

August 22 - Carlos Beltran belts a grand slam and knocks in six runs, but the Royals lose a slugfest to the White Sox at the The K, 13-12.

September 11 - All MLB games are canceled due to the terrorist attacks in New York, Pennsylvania and Washington, DC.

October 7 - Another grand slam for Beltran. The Royals' outfielder also knocks in six runs as KC ends the season with a 10-4 win at Detroit. The Royals finish with a record of 65-97 and a last place finish in the AL Central.

December 17 - The Royals sign free-agent pitcher Darrell May.

December 18 - The Royals sign free-agent outfielder Chuck Knoblauch.

2002

January 10 - Pitcher Paul Byrd signs a free-agent contract with the Royals.

April 1 - The Royals the lose the season opener to the Twins at The K, 8-6.

April 9 - Chuck Knoblauch hits a grand slam at Fenway Park, but the Royals lose to the Red Sox, 8-4.

April 29 - Tony Muser is tossed from the game for arguing a check swing strike, but the Royals still win, 4-0, as Jeff Suppan tosses a two-hitter at the Tigers. Following the game, Muser

> It's very disappointing to lose one-hundred (games). We (the 2002 Kansas City Royals) have more talent than that.
> **Carlos Beltran**

is fired as the club's manager. The Royals' Bullpen coach, John Mizerock, is named interim manager.

May 15 - Tony Pena is hired as the Royals new manager.

> *These things happen. I'm not ashamed. I did the best I could possibly do.*
> **Tony Muser**
> **after being fired**

July 13 - Kansas City signs their first round draft pick, Zack Greinke.

July 21 - Carlos Beltran belts a grand slam as the Royals defeat Cleveland at Kauffman Stadium, 13-12, in 10 innings.

> *I am the new DJ. I play the music. You are to dance. If you don't know how to dance, get off of the dance floor.*
> **Tony Pena**
> **on being named the**
> **Royals new manager**

August 10 - Tampa Bay hits six home runs and buries the Royals, 13-6, at Kauffman Stadium.

August 14 - Mike Sweeney steals home against the Yanks, but the New Yorkers still prevail at Kauffman Stadium, 3-2 in 14 innings.

September 29 - The Indians defeat Kansas City, 7-3, in Cleveland, and for the first time in franchise history, the Royals finish the season with 100 losses. Their 62-100 record still lands them ahead of the Tigers, who finish with 106 losses.

November 25 - The Royals place SS Neifi Perez on waivers and lose him to San Francisco Giants.

2003

January 10 - The Royals sign free-agent utility man Desi Relaford.

March 11 - The Royals release outfielder Mark Quinn.

March 31 - By the flip of a coin, Runelvys Hernandez wins the Opening Day pitching assignment for KC, and then blanks the White Sox, 3-0, at Kauffman Stadium.

April 11 - Runelvys Hernandez wins his third game of the season and Mike MacDougal picks up his sixth save as the Royals win in Cleveland, 1-0.

April 12 - Raul Ibanez homers as the Royals win their record-setting ninth straight game at the start of the season. They do it in Cleveland, stopping the Tribe, 5-2.

April 15 - Ninth-inning lightning! The Royals score four times in the ninth inning to defeat the White Sox, 8-5 in Chicago. The game was delayed in the eighth when fans stormed the field to attack umpire Laz Diaz.

April 24 - Mike Sweeney homers as the Royals top the Twins at Kauffman, 2-1. Chris George wins his third game of the season as KC improves to 16-3.

May 9 - The Royals drop a doubleheader to the Orioles at Kauffman Stadium, 15-5 and 5-4.

June 4 - Kansas City purchases pitcher Jose Lima from Newark of the Independent Atlantic League.

June 27 - The Royals defeat the Cardinals at Kauffman Stadium, 6-3, the team's 10th win in their last 12 games.

July 10 - Wes Obermueller and Alejandro Machado are traded to Milwaukee for Curt Leskanic.

July 13 - Home runs from Angel Berroa and Aaron Guiel led the way as the Royals defeat the Rangers in Texas, 8-2. The win gives first place Kansas City a seven-game lead in the Central Division at the All-Star break.

July 28 - Kansas City trades Jeremy Hill to the New York Mets for relief pitcher Graeme Lloyd.

August 6 - Welcome back. The Royals sign free-agent pitcher Kevin Appier.

August 11 - KC and the Yankees hit 19 doubles combined at Kauffman Stadium to establish a new American League record. The Royals win, 12-9.

August 21 - The Royals lose to the Twins in Minnesota, 4-3, and fall out of first place.

August 25 - Kansas City sends Trey Dyson, Kieran Mattison, and cash to Cleveland for pitcher Brian Anderson and a player to be named later.

Royals' shortstop Angel Berroa, the 2003 American League Rookie of the Year, prepares to tag out a Detroit runner.

August 26 - The Royals get outfielder Rondell White from the Padres for Chris Tierney and Brian Sanches.

August 28 - Mike Sweeney hits an RBI single in the bottom of the 11th inning to give the Royals a 6-5 win over Texas, moving the team back into first place in the AL Central.

August 31 - The Royals lose to the Angels at Kauffman Stadium to fall a game and a half behind the White Sox.

September 28 - In the final game of the season, Chicago defeats Kansas City 5-1 at Kauffman Stadium. The Royals finish at 83-79, seven games behind the White Sox. The winning record is the team's first since 1994.

November 10 - Royals' shortstop Angel Berroa is the American League winner of the Jackie Robinson Rookie-of-the-Year Award, the fourth Royals player to win the award.

November 11 - Kansas City signs free-agent first baseman Calvin Pickering.

November 12 - Tony Pena is named American League Manager of the Year.

December 10 - The Royals sign free-agent catcher Benito Santiago to a two-year contract.

2004

January 6 - The Royals sign free-agent outfielder Juan Gonzalez to a one-year contract.

January 25 - The Royals sign free-agent utility player Jed Hansen.

April 5 - The Royals defeat the White Sox in the season opener at Kauffman Stadium, 9-7. Carlos Beltran wins the game with a walk-off home run.

April 20 - Matt Stairs hits a grand slam and knocks in six runs as the Royals win in Cleveland, 15-5.

> *I've always been a Kansas City Royal. I want to end my career here like George Brett did and like Mike Sweeney will do, but I understand this game is a business.*
> **Carlos Beltran**
> before the 2004 season

June 11 - The Royals sign their 2004 first round draft pick, Billy Butler.

June 21 - Pitcher Jason Grimsley is traded to the Orioles for pitcher Denny Bautista.

June 24 - Beltran heads south. Kansas City trades Carlos Beltran to Houston in a three-team deal. KC receives Minor League third baseman Mark Teahen and pitcher Mike Wood from Oakland, and catcher John Buck from the Astros. The Athletics get pitcher Octavio Dotel from the Astros.

July 20 - Tony Pena is ejected from the game for arguing about balls and strikes. Baltimore clobbers the Royals at Kauffman Stadium, 12-3.

August 4 - Brian Anderson tosses at two-hitter as the Royals rout the White Sox, 11-0, at Kauffman Stadium.

August 13 - The Royals hit two grand slams against the A's in Oakland and win easily, 10-3.

August 27 - The Mariners blast six home runs against the Royals and defeat KC in Seattle, 7-5.

September 9 - The Royals rip the Tigers in Detroit, setting a team record for most hits in a game with 26, and also most runs scored in a game to win, 26-5. Joe Randa leads the hit parade for KC, slamming six hits and scoring six runs.

October 3 - The Royals drop the final game of the season to the White Sox, 5-0, the 104th loss of the year. Once again, the team finishes in last place.

December 16 - Kansas City sends catcher Benito Santiago and cash to Pittsburgh for pitcher Leo Nunez.

2005

February 24 - The Royals sign free-agent outfielder Matt Diaz.

April 4 - The Tigers crush the Royals in the season opener at Detroit, 11-2. Jose Lima is the losing pitcher for KC.

April 30 - Ken Harvey hits a grand slam as the Royals top the Indians 8-1 in Cleveland.

May 10 - Tony Pena resigns as the manager of the Royals. Bob Schaefer was named the interim manager for the team.

> *I can't take it any more.*
> **Tony Pena**
> when he resigned as the Royals' manager

May 31 - Buddy Bell is hired as the new manager of the Royals.

July 27 - It takes 13 innings, but the Royals defeat the White Sox 6-5 at Kauffman Stadium. KC doesn't win again for more than three weeks.

> *Realistically, what we really expect out of Buddy this year is to get this team playing to its truest talent level and I think our record is not an indicator of how much talent we have on this club.*
> **Royals President Dan Glass**
> on hiring Buddy Bell to manage the Royals

July 28 - The Devil Rays defeat the Royals in Tampa Bay, 10-5, the first of 19 straight losses for KC.

August 5 - Relief pitcher Jeremy Affeldt gives up two runs in the eighth inning at Kauffman Stadium as the Royals drop a close one to Oakland, 5-4.

August 6 - The A's rap out 18 hits and easily defeat the Royals at Kauffman Stadium, 16-1.

August 10 - Royals' manager Buddy Bell is ejected from the game as the Royals lose to Cleveland at Kauffman Stadium, 6-1.

August 19 - The Royals lose for a club-record 19th straight time, losing at Oakland, 4-0.

August 20 - Finally. The Royals end their club-record 19-game losing streak by beating the A's in Oakland, 2-1. Pitcher Jose Lima celebrates by pouring and sharing Dom Perignon Champagne with his teammates.

> *This win is like winning a playoff game. We're a young team, we stuck together and took it like a man. It's tough to stay tough, but we did it.*
>
> **Jose Lima**
> when the Royals ended their 19-game losing streak

September 30 - Zack Greinke gives up seven runs in four innings to lose his 17th game of the season. The Blue Jays top KC in Toronto, 10-1.

October 2 - With a 7-2 loss at Toronto, the worst season in the franchise's history comes to a merciful end. With a final record of 56-106, the Royals finish 43 games behind the division-winning White Sox.

December 7 - The Royals trade Jonah Bayliss and Chad Blackwell to the Pirates for pitcher Mark Redman.

December 16 - The Royals sign free-agent second baseman Mark Grudzielanek.

2006

January 6 - The Royals sign free-agent outfielder Reggie Sanders.

February 26 - Zack Greinke leaves the Royals' training facilities in Arizona and returns to his home in Orlando. It was later disclosed that Greinke was dealing with an anxiety disorder.

March 28 - The Royals claim Tony Graffanino off waivers from the Red Sox.

April 3 - The Royals drop the season opener to the Tigers at Kauffman Stadium, 3-1.

April 17 - Zack Greinke returns to the Royals' spring training facility in Arizona and begins pitching again.

If I didn't think we would win a world championship in Kansas City, there is no way I would commit myself and my family to this environment.

Dayton Moore
on being named the
Royals' GM in 2006

May 31 - The Royals' general manager Allard Baird is fired.

June 8 - Dayton Moore is hired as the Royals general manager.

June 11 - The Royals purchase pitcher Brandon Duckworth from the Pittsburgh Pirates.

June 20 - Kansas City trades pitcher J.P. Howell to Tampa Bay for outfielder Joey Gathright infielder Fernando Cortez.

Royals' second baseman Mark Grudzielanek won the 2006 American League Gold Glove award.

Mike Sweeney

July 5 - Kansas City places Aaron Guiel on waivers and the outfielder is claimed by the Yankees.

July 24 - The Royals trade pitcher Mike MacDougal to the White Sox for Tyler Lumsden and Dan Cortes.

> *I was actually hoping the Royals would pick me. It was the main team I wanted to go to. Their colors are Royal Blue and that's my favorite color.*
>
> **Zack Greinke**

July 31 - The Royals trade outfielder Matt Stairs to the Texas Rangers for Jose Diaz, and trade pitchers Jeremy Affeldt and Denny Bautista to the Colorado Rockies in exchange for Ryan Shealy and Scott Dohmann.

August 10 - The Royals rough up Boston's Curt Schilling for 10 extra-base hits at Kauffman Stadium to tie an American League record. KC wins, 5-4.

August 23 - After scoring 10 runs in the first inning, the Royals blow the game when pitcher Joe Nelson gives up four runs in the ninth inning. KC loses to the Tribe in 10 innings at Kauffman Stadium, 15-13.

September 22 - Zack Greinke returns and pitches one inning for the Royals in relief. KC loses to the Tigers at Kauffman Stadium, 7-3.

October 1 - It takes 12 innings, but the Royals defeat the Tigers in Detroit, 10-8, to complete a three-game sweep and finish the season with a record of 62-100. It's the fourth time in five seasons the Royals lose at least 100 games.

November 3 - Mark Grudzielanek wins the American League second baseman Gold Glove.

December 7 - The Royals select Joakim Soria from San Diego Padres in the Rule 5 draft.

> *This is a new year, and I'm excited. There's a new atmosphere in the clubhouse.*
>
> **Mike Sweeney**
> before the 2007 season

December 13 - The Royals sign free-agent pitcher Gil Meche to a five-year contract worth $55 million.

2007

February 22 - Radio announcer Denny Matthews is selected as the 2007 recipient of the Ford C. Frick award, which is presented annually for major contributions to baseball broadcasting.

April 2 - Royals win the season opener at Kauffman against the Red Sox, 7-1. Gil Meche gets his first win for Kansas City. Also, the Buck O'Neil legacy seat debuts at Kauffman Stadium. A red seat was placed behind home plate to honor the legendary ball player. Every game, a person is selected from community nominees to sit in the seat formerly reserved for O'Neil.

Gil Meche

May 10 - Oakland tees off on the Royals pitchers at Kauffman Stadium, hitting six home runs. The A's rout Kansas City, 17-3.

June 30 – The Royals lose to Chicago, 3-1, but finish with a 15-12 record for the month of June, the team's first winning month since July, 2003.

July 3 - Billy Butler knocks in six runs as the Royals pound the Mariners at Kauffman Stadium, 17-3.

July 31 - The Royals trade pitcher Octavio Dotel to the Braves for pitcher Kyle Davies.

> *It was a mess when I got here and for a while they were talking about the GM (Allard Baird) getting fired and he eventually got fired.*
> **Buddy Bell**

August 1 - Royals' manager Buddy Bell announces that he will retire at the end of the season.

September 12 - Royals defeat the Minnesota Twins, 6-3, and win their 63rd game of the season. The win guarantees the team will not lose 100 games for the first time since 2003.

> *I'm so grateful for everything you've done to help me develop into the player—and more importantly the man—I've become.*
> **Mike Sweeney**
> thanking the Royals before his final game in Kansas City

September 30 - Mike Sweeney plays his final game for Kansas City as the Royals lose the season finale to Cleveland at Kauffman Stadium, 4-2, and finish with a record of 69-93. The Royals' Captain receives standing ovations before each of his at-bats. David DeJesus finishes season with the record for the most hit by pitches in a single season with 23.

> *I'm a hungry guy. I do not like to lose. I like to start from the ground up and build, and build in such a way that it's going to be maintained for many years to come.*
> **Trey Hillman**
> **on being named**
> **Royals' manager**

October 19 - Trey Hillman is hired as the 15th full-time manager of the Kansas City Royals.

October 30 - Mike Sweeney is granted free agency.

November 15 - Mike Sweeney is named the 2007 winner of the Hutch Award, which is given to the MLB player who exemplifies both on and off the field the competitive desire and fighting spirit of baseball great Fred Hutchinson.

December 4 - The Royals sign free-agent outfielder Jose Guillen.

December 6 - The Royals introduce a new alternate jersey, which is designed after the powder blue uniforms worn by the Royals from 1973 to 1991 on the road.

December 27 - The Royals sign free-agent catcher Miguel Olivo.

2008

March 26 - Justin Huber is traded to the Padres for a player to be determined later and money.

March 31 - Royals open the season at Detroit and win 5-4 in 11 innings.

April 8 - Kauffman Stadium's new scoreboard makes its debut at the home opener against the New York Yankees. It is 84 feet wide by 105 feet tall, the largest high-definition LED display in the world at the time. The Royals beat the Yankees, 5-2.

Zack Greinke

May 27 - Mark Teahen hits a three-run, inside-the-park-home run in the bottom of the ninth to tie the game with the Twins, but the Royals still lose in 12 innings, 4-3.

May 30 - The Royals claim Brayan Pena off waivers from the Braves.

June 6 - The Royals trade Angel Berroa, the 2003 AL Rookie of the Year, to the Dodgers for Juan Rivera.

June 30 - Migel Olivo hits a two-out, pinch-hit home run in the ninth inning for the Royals at Baltimore to tie the score, and KC wins in 11 innings, 6-5.

> *The Royals stuck with me. I'm glad they did. I probably tried to get traded a couple of times back in the day. But they decided to keep me anyway.*
> **Zack Greinke**

August 3 - Miguel Olivo is ejected after charging the mound when he is hit by a pitch, and Zack Greinke is ejected after hitting a batter two innings later. Manager Trey Hillman is also ejected. Kansas City still wins easily, 14 -3, over the White Sox at home.

September 28 - The Royals finish season with a loss at Minnesota, 6-0, and a record of 75-87, good for fourth place in the AL Central.

October 30 - The Royals acquire Mike Jacobs from the Florida Marlins for pitcher Leo Nunez.

November 18 - The Royals trade pitcher Ramon Ramirez to the Red Sox for Coco Crisp.

December 13 – The Royals sign free-agent pitcher Kyle Farnsworth.

2009

January 26 - The Royals sign pitcher Zack Greinke to a four-year contract extension.

April 7 - The bullpen gives up three runs in the eighth inning as Kansas City drops the season opener to the White Sox in Chicago, 4-2.

April 10 - The "New K" opens. With the $250 million renovation complete, Kauffman Stadium hosts its first game. The Yankees spoil the day though, and defeat the Royals, 4-1.

April 14 - John Buck hits a grand slam at Kauffman Stadium as the Royals defeat the Indians, 9-3.

April 17 - Mark Teahen raps out five hits in Texas as the Royals pound the Rangers, 12-3.

July 10 - The Royals send pitchers Derrick Saito and Dan Cortes to the Mariners for SS Yuni Betancourt.

July 27 - The Royals top the Orioles in Baltimore, 5-3, as Billy Butler raps five hits.

August 25 - Good stuff. Zack Greinke fans 15 Indians to set a new club record for strikeouts in a game. The Royals top Cleveland, 6-2.

August 30 - Zack Greinke tosses a one-hitter in Seattle as the Royals defeat the Mariners, 3-0.

October 4 - The Twins clobber the Royals, 13-4, in the final game of the season. Kansas City finishes with a record of 65-97—last place in the AL Central Division.

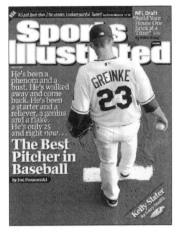

Zack Greinke graced the cover of Sports Illustrated the year he won the Cy Young Award.

November 6 - Mark Teahen is sent to the White Sox for Chris Getz and Josh Fields. Kansas City also sends cash to Chicago.

November 17 - Zack Greinke is named the 2009 American League Cy Young Award winner. Greinke finished the 2009 season with a 16-8 record, 242 strikeouts, and a league-best 2.16 ERA.

December 11 - The Royals sign free-agent catcher Jason Kendall to a two-year, six million-dollar contract.

2010

January 8 - The Royals sign free-agent outfielder Scott Podsednik.

January 25 - The Royals sign free-agent outfielder Rick Ankiel.

April 5 – The Royals lose the season opener at home to Tigers, 8-4.

May 13 – After the Royals defeat the Indians 6-4, Manager Trey Hillman is fired. Special Advisor to the team, Ned Yost, is named interim manager for the remainder of the year.

June 16 - MLB Commissioner Bud Selig announces that the 2012 All-Star Game will be at Kauffman Stadium.

July 22 - Royals trade third baseman Alberto Callaspo to the Angels for pitchers Sean O'Sullivan and Will Smith.

July 29 - Royals trade outfielder Scott Podsednik to the Dodgers for catcher Lucas May and pitcher Elisaul Pimentel.

July 31 - Rick Ankiel and Kyle Farnsworth are traded to the Braves for pitcher Tim Collins, outfielder Gregor Blanco, and pitcher Jesse Chavez. Also, Ned Yost signs a two-contract extension as the Royals' manager.

August 13 - The Royals trade outfielder Jose Guillen to the Giants for pitcher Kevin Pucetas.

September 12 - Billy Butler sets franchise record of at least 1 hit in 97 consecutive series, but the Royals lose to the White Sox in Chicago, 12-6.

September 13 - Willie Bloomquist traded to the Reds for a player to be named later and cash.

September 30 - Joakim Soria notches his 43rd save of the season as the Royals top the Rays at Kauffman Stadium, 3-2.

October 3 - Royals end their season with a 67-95 record, losing their last game at home 2-3 against Tampa Bay. They finish last in the American League Central Division for the 6th time in seven years.

> *Where I'm at in my career . . . I'm saying, 'Am I ever going to get to the playoffs? Am I ever going to be on a team like that?'*"
> **Billy Butler**

November 10 - The Royals trade David DeJesus to the A's for pitcher Vin Mazarro and pitcher Justin Marks.

December 8 - The Royals sign free-agent outfielder Jeff Francoeur to a one-year contract.

December 10 - The Royals sign free-agent outfielder Melky Cabrera.

December 19 - Zack has to pack. The Royals trade Cy Young Award winning pitcher Zack Greinke and shortstop Yuniesky Betancourt to the Brewers for shortstop Alcides Escobar, outfielder Lorenzo Cain, pitcher Jake Odorizzi, and pitcher Jeremy Jeffress.

2011

January 6 - Royals' pitcher Gil Meche announces retirement and walks away from the final season of his five-year, $55 million contract.

January 15 - The Royals sign free-agent pitcher Bruce Chen.

March 25 - Mike Sweeney is signed to a one-day contract that allows him to retire as a Kansas City Royal.

March 28 - Matt Treanor is traded from the Rangers to the Royals for cash.

March 31 - Royals open the season at home against the Angels and lose, 4-2.

Joakim Soria

May 7 - Eric Hosmer collects his first Major League hit, a fifth-inning single, and the Royals defeat the A's at Kauffman Stadium, 4-3.

May 27 - The Royals acquire Felipe Paulino from the Rockies for cash.

July 20 - Wilson Betemit is traded for the Tigers' Antonio Cruz and Julio Rodriguez.

July 30 - Mike Aviles is traded to the Red Sox for Kendal Volz and Yamaico Navarro.

August 7 - Alex Gordon sets franchise record of 18 outfield assists in a single season.

> *I love it here (Kansas City). I love the fans. I love everything about this place.*
> **Alex Gordon**

August 10 - Royals' catcher Salvador Perez makes his Major League debut. The Royals lose at Tampa Bay, 8-7.

August 31 - Matt Treanor is sent to the Rangers for cash.

September 21 - Billy Butler hits his 40th double making the Royals the 4th team in history to have four players with 40 doubles. KC loses to Detroit at home, 6-3.

September 27 - Kila Ka'aihue is traded to the A's for Phillip Hollingsworth.

September 29 - Royals finish season with a 71- 91 record, losing their final game 0-1 at Minnesota. They again finish 4th in the AL Central.

November 1 - Alex Gordon wins the American League Gold Glove for the outfield.

November 7 - Melky Cabrera is traded to the Giants for Jonathan Sanchez and Ryan Verdugo.

Ned Yost became the Royals' manager in 2010.

November 23 - Royals re-sign Bruce Chen to a two-year deal.

November 29 - The Royals sign free-agent pitcher Jonathan Broxton.

December 20 - The Royals sign free-agent shortstop Yuniesky Betancourt.

2012

January 8 - Legendary groundskeeper George Toma is inducted as part of the inaugural class of the Major League Baseball Groundskeepers Hall of Fame.

February 27 - The Royals and catcher Salvador Perez agree to a five-year contract extension.

April 6 - Royals open the season at home against the Angels. And lose, 5-0.

June 21 - Sean O'Sullivan is traded to the Blue Jays for cash.

July 10 - The 83rd edition of the Major League Baseball All-Star Game was held at Kauffman Stadium, the third time the Mid-summer Classic had been played in Kansas City. Billy was the Royals representative in the game, which was won by the National League, 8-0.

July 20 - Jonathan Sanchez is traded for the Rockies' Jeremy Guthrie.

July 31 - Jonathan Broxton is traded to the Reds for Donnie Joseph and J.C. Sulbaran.

August 31 - Royals go 17-11 in August, for their first winning month of August since 2000 when they went 15-14, and their best since 1991 when they went 18-11.

September 18 - Billy Butler sets a career high with his 97th RBI in a 2-3 loss to the Chicago White Sox.

September 19 -Alcides Escobar collects his 165th hit of the season against the White Sox, setting a new season record for the Royals for hits by a short-stop. The Royals win, 3-0.

September 21 - George Toma is inducted into the Royals Hall of Fame. Toma was the head groundskeeper for the Royals from 1969-1995.

Eric Hosmer

Eric Hosmer (35) celebrates with Billy Butler (16) and Alex Gordon (4) after hitting a three-run home run in a 2013 game.

September 22 - Billy Butler drove in his 100th RBI in the game against the Indians. This is a new career best for him in a season and he is also the first Royal to reach the 100-RBI mark since Carlos Beltran in 2003.

October 3 - Royals finish season with a 72- 90 record, losing their final game to Detroit at home, 1-0, and claim a third-place finish in the AL Central.

October 26 - Chris Volstad claimed off waivers from the Cubs.

October 31 - Brandon Sisk is traded to the Angels for Ervin Santana.

> *Look, I don't know if Ned's the perfect manager. But I know one thing: After the last game in Chicago, the players freaking love Ned Yost.*
> **GM Dayton Moore**

November 2 - Brett Hayes is claimed off waivers from the Marlins.

November 20 - Royals sign Jeremy Guthrie to a three-year contract.

November 28 - Clint Robinson and Vin Mazzaro traded to the Pirates for Luis Rico and Luis Santos.

December 9 - Wil Myers, Jake Odorizzi, Mike Montgomery, and Patrick Leonard are traded to Tampa Bay for Wade Davis, James Shields, and Elliot Johnson.

December 31 - Free-agent Miguel Tejeda signs a minor league contract with an invitation to attend major league camp.

2013

January 25 - The Royals claim George Kottaras off waivers from Oakland.

February 12 - The Royals acquire second baseman Elliot Johnson from Tampa Bay.

April 1 - The Royals lose the season opener to the White Sox in Chicago, 1-0.

April 10 - The Royals shutout the Twins at Kauffman Stadium, 3-0. James Shields records his first win as a Royal.

> *What are you asking me to do? Take my belt off and spank them? Yell at them? Scream at them?*
>
> **Ned Yost**
> **during the Royals slump**
> **in May, 2013**

April 19 - The Royals game at Boston is postponed as the city goes into lockdown during the search for the Boston Marathon bombers.

May 5 - The Royals defeat the White Sox at home in 10 innings, 6-5. The win moves the team's record to 17-10.

May 6 - The start of a swoon. The Royals give up a run in the ninth inning and lose to the White Sox in 11 innings, 2-1. The Royals start a losing trend that sees them lose 19 of 22 games.

July 5 - Outfielder Jeff Francoeur is released.

July 31 - The Royals trade Kyle Smith to the Astros for outfielder Justin Maxwell.

Sal Perez and Greg Holland celebrate another save.

August 1 - KC defeats the Twins in Minnesota, 7-2, the team's ninth straight win.

August 11 - The Royals purchase infielder Jamey Carroll from the Twins.

August 14 - The Royals purchase infielder Emilio Bonifacio from the Blue Jays.

> *In a small way, I feel like we've won the World Series. What I'm saying, I mean, look, 'World Series' is the wrong term. But I feel very, very good about where our organization is. It means a lot to me.*
> **GM Dayton Moore**
> after the 2013 season

September 4 - The Royals use eight pitchers against Seattle, the most in club history for a single game. KC still loses at Kauffman Stadium, 6-4.

September 18 - Alcides Escobar steals home against Cleveland as the Royals win at Kauffman Stadium, 7-2.

September 22 - In the final home game of the season, Justin Maxwell crushes a grand slam in the 10th inning—the Royals beat Texas, 4-0.

September 29 - The Royals defeat the White Sox in Chicago 4-1 to finish the season with an 86-76 record, the most wins by the team since 1989. Greg Holland sets a club record by notching his 47th save of the season.

November 21 - The Royals sign free-agent pitcher Jason Vargas.

November 26 - The Royals sell catcher George Kottaras to the Cubs.

December 5 - Royals' pitcher Will Smith is traded to the Milwaukee Brewers for outfielder Norichika Aoki.

December 16 - The Royals sign free-agent second baseman Omar Infante.

December 18 - The Royals trade outfielder David Lough to Baltimore for third baseman Danny Valencia.

2014

February 1 - The Royals re-sign free-agent pitcher Bruce Chen.

February 10 - The Royals release second baseman Emilio Bonifacio.

Royals
Players
Trivia

George Brett

George Brett

I have never seen a player who could dominate a baseball game, or a series, or a month of series, the way that George Brett can dominate. Brett is an amazing hitter—strong, with tremendous bat control, excellent command of the strike zone. His swing is a thing of beauty.

Bill James, 1988
The Bill James Historical Baseball Abstract

If you saw him play, then you know how extraordinarily remarkable his baseball talents were. Running, fielding, throwing and most of all, hitting. His career was filled with clutch hits, pennant-winning home runs and amazing batting exhibitions that covered long stretches of time. George Brett was a great baseball player, and with his induction ceremony on July 25, 1999, in Cooperstown, New York, a most deserving Hall-of-Famer.

Brett helped make the Royals champions, not just with his hitting (which was enough to make most teams champions), but also with his heart, spirit and competitive nature. His greatest season was 1985 when he stormed through the final two weeks of the season, literally carrying the Royals on his back as he led them to the division title, American League pennant, and then to the world championship.

Brett's career accomplishments, the number of hits, RBIs, HRs, etc., are overwhelming, but he was more than statistics. Brett was, as Detroit manager called him, Superman—the guy who got the big hit.

He was, and always will be, Kansas City's favorite baseball player.

1. Where did Brett go to high school?

2. Brett got his first Major League hit off of which White Sox pitcher on August 2, 1973?

3. Who gave up Brett's first Major League home run?

4. How many times did Brett lead the American League in triples?

5. How many times did Brett lead the American League in doubles?

6. Brett twice collected 200 or more hits in a single season. What two years were they?

7. What season did Brett switch to first base?

8. Who gave up Brett's 2,000th hit?

9. Who gave up Brett's 3,000th hit, and when and where did he get it?

10. What happened after he got the 3,000th hit?

11. How many pinch-hit home runs did Brett hit for the Royals?

12. Who was the Texas pitcher that ended Brett's 30-game hitting streak in 1980?

13. In which stadium did Brett collect his 1,500th hit?

14. Brett joined an exclusive group when he hit his 300th career home run, being one of six players to hit 300 home runs and have 3,000 hits. Who was the pitcher that gave up Brett's 300th home run?

15. Who are the other five players that accomplished the 300-3,000 feat?

16. Who gave up Brett's 200th home run in 1986?

17. In 1975 George collected 11 consecutive hits off this California pitcher, and ended the season 12 of 14 against him. Who was the pitcher?

18. How many consecutive All-Star teams was George selected to?

19. How many consecutive All-Star Games was George selected to start?

20. How many times did Brett steal home in his career?

21. George's brother Ken played with the Royals for parts of two seasons. What seasons were they?

22. How many hits did George have when he retired?

23. Who gave up George's last hit, and where did he get it?

24. How many games did Brett play in?

25. What is Brett's career batting average?

26. Who were the other two players chosen by the Baseball Writers to go into the Hall of Fame with Brett?

Hal McRae

Charlie Lau means one hundred grand.

Hal McRae, 1976
on what Hitting Coach
Charlie Lau meant to him

It was my biggest disappointment in baseball. We should have won the World Series that year, and everybody in baseball knew it.

Hal McRae
on the 1977 Royals

The ultimate when it comes to designated hitters. Hal set the parameters for the special hitting role, not just in Kansas City, but in all of Major League Baseball. When he became the Royals DH, the team became a consistent winner.

Hard-hitting, hard-nosed and hard playing, Hal never held back throughout his career. He was almost single-handedly responsible for the new slide rule at second base (still known today as the "McRae rule") that keeps sliding runners at the bag, not the second baseman or shortstop. His teammates called him "Mr. Ribbie" for his penchant to knock in big runs; the Royals Stadium scoreboard called his at bats "Big Mac Attacks."

Hal's managerial career with the Royals shouldn't have ended the way it did, especially since he was a winner at that, too. McRae was named to three All-Star squads during his career, but he'll always be considered an All-Star in Kansas City.

1. Hal played baseball at what university?

2. When and with what team did Hal make his Major League debut?

3. Hal led the American League in doubles twice. What years did he lead and how many did he hit?

4. How many times did Hal lead the AL in RBIs?

Hal McRae

5. How many career hits does Hal have?

6. What pitcher was traded with Hal from the Reds to the Royals, and what two Royals players were involved in the trade?

7. What position did Hal hold with the Royals in 1987?

8. Hal lost the batting title to George Brett on the last day of the season in 1976 by .001 points. What was Hal's average?

9. How many times in his career did Hal hit .300 or better?

10. Hal played in four different World Series. How many home runs did he hit in the Fall Classic?

11. What was his batting average in the 1985 World Series?

12. What is his lifetime World Series batting average?

Frank White

If any one player in the American League owned a position defensively throughout the 1970s and 1980s, it was Frank White at second base. Kansas City's hometown product set the standard at his position, collecting Gold Gloves as easily as he collected ground balls. Overlooked for offensive output early in his career, Frank powered up and became an important offensive force in the Royals lineup the last half of his career.

The most successful graduate of the Royals' Baseball Academy, Frank led the league in fielding percentage three times, played 62 straight games without an error in 1977, and hit 22 home runs two years in row, 1985-86. But like Brett, Frank was more than statistics. His worth to the team, and Kansas City, extended past the boundaries of the playing field.

Frank returned to Kansas City as the Royals' first base coach in 1997.

1. When and where did Frank White play in his first game for KC?

2. What position did he play in his first game?

3. When did he get his first hit?

4. When did he play his first game at second base?

5. When and off whom did he hit his first home run?

6. How many Gold Gloves did Frank win?

7. When did Frank win his first Gold Glove?

8. How many Gold Gloves did Frank win in a row?

9. What year was he named to his first AL All-Star game?

10. How many All-Star games was he selected for?

11. Frank earned a starting role in only one All-Star game. What was the year?

12. How many career hits does Frank have?

Frank White

Willie Wilson

The fastest of all Royals? Probably, and then some. As the Royals' top pick in the June 1974 Free Agent Draft, Wilson signed with Kansas City, passing on a college scholarship to play football at the University of Maryland.

Willie used his speed well, but he was more than just a runner. His defensive ability in the outfield was not only exciting, but also earned him a Gold Glove; his hitting earned him an American League batting championship. His talents were many, but he'll always be remembered as a base stealer, and that's okay. Remember also his knack for getting on base, hitting inside-the-park home runs, and thrilling Kansas City fans with a level of play matched by few who have worn the Royals uniform.

1. When did Willie play in his first game for the Royals?

2. How many times did Willie lead the AL in stolen bases?

3. Willie holds the Royals team record for triples in a season. How many, and in what year did he set this record?

4. Willie was the second player ever to collect 100 hits from both sides of the plate (batting both right-handed and left-handed) during a season. Who was the first player to accomplish this?

5. In the 1980 season Willie was the first Major Leaguer ever to accomplish this feat. What was it?

6. How many times did Willie lead the American League in Triples?

7. How many times did Willie lead the AL in runs scored?

8. How many batting titles did Willie win?

9. How many All-Star games was Willie selected for?

10. How many stolen bases did Willie collect in the 1985 World Series?

11. What two teams did Willie play for after he left the Royals?

Willie Wilson

Bret Saberhagen

The greatest Royals pitcher of all time? If you're picking one, it has to be Saberhagen. The two-time Cy Young Award winner showed Kansas City fans some of the finest pitching in the American League from 1984-91.

Bret loved pressure games for the Royals. The bigger the game, the better he pitched. In the pennant race, ALCS, or World Series, Saberhagen delivered. A two-time All-Star selection for the American League squad, Bret fought through a couple of disappointing seasons and seemed destined to play out his career in KC, much like Splittorff and Leonard. His unexpected trade and departure from Kansas City still sits uneasy with many fans.

1. Where did Saberhagen attend high school?

2. True or false: Saberhagen pitched a no-hitter in the Los Angeles city high school championship game.

Saberhagen pitches during Game 3 of the 1985 World Series.

3. What position was Saberhagen originally drafted to play?

4. What round was he drafted in?

5. When and against whom did Saberhagen make his Major League debut?

6. How old was he in his debut game?

7. He earned his first start and victory against what team?

8. What team did the Royals trade Saberhagen to and for what players?

9. How many games did Saberhagen win in the 1985 World Series?

10. How many games did Saberhagen win in his career with the Royals?

11. True or False: In addition to the Cy Young Award, Saberhagen also won a Gold Glove in 1989.

12. When and against what team did Saberhagen pitch his no-hitter?

Bo Jackson

Baseball player playing football, or football player pretending to play baseball? Regardless of his talent, expertise and speed, Bo Jackson knew how to create excitement. Whether he was sending an opposing pitcher's fastball to the back end of the bullpen at Royals Stadium or viciously striking out and then snapping the bat across his leg like a twig, Bo knew baseball. Forget about the football "hobby" and the career-ending hip injury. Bo gave Kansas City a true media superstar.

His shooting-star career was highly scrutinized and, in the end, lamented. He wasn't in the game—at least wearing a Royals uniform—long enough, but even in his brief time (four full seasons with KC), his talent, like George Brett's, made fans feel the Royals always had a chance to win.

1. Who gave up Bo Jackson's first Major League hit on September 2, 1986?

2. Which Seattle pitcher gave up Jackson's first Major League home run? When and where did Bo hit it?

3. During his career at Kansas City, Bo only once led the American League in a hitting category. What was the category, how many and what year?

4. Did Bo ever win a Gold Glove? If so, when?

5. In 1988, Bo became the first Royal ever to accomplish this feat of speed and power in the same season. He repeated it in 1989. What did he do?

6. In what year did Bo win college football's Heisman Trophy?

7. What was Bo's uniform number when he played for the Los Angeles Raiders?

8. Bo homered in four consecutive at bats in 1990. Who was the pitcher that gave up the fourth home run?

9. What year did Bo win the All-Star Game MVP?

10. Which National League pitcher gave up a homer to Bo in that All-Star game?

11. Bo joined Willie Mays as the only other player ever to do these two things in an All-Star game. What are they?

Bo Jackson

Amos Otis

Amos Otis

The Royals first real superstar, Otis came to Kansas City (he was stolen, really, for the Mets didn't know what they had) and filled the spaces of center field with grace, speed and Gold Glove defensive skill. He always played deep, possessing an uncanny knack for coming in on a ball to make the play. Otis added speed and average at the plate, and peppered the opposing teams with occasional power. He led the American League in doubles twice with 36 in 1970 and 40 in 1976. He tied an American League record by stealing seven bases in two consecutive games in 1975, and finished his career with 341 steals.

Always a big performer in the big games, Otis gave an MVP performance in the 1980 World Series, leading the team with a .478 average. He hit .279 in the four championship series against the Yankees.

1. What team did Otis start his Major League career with?

2. How did the Royals acquire him?

3. What year did Amos lead the American League in stolen bases?

4. Which one of Otis' teammates finished second in stolen bases that year?

5. What year did Otis start in the All-Star game?

6. How many All-Star games was he selected for?

7. On September 7, 1971, Otis accomplished something that hadn't happened in the American League in 44 years. What did he do and against what team?

8. When did he win his first Gold Glove?

9. How many Gold Gloves did Otis win?

10. What team did Otis finish his career with?

Dan Quisenberry

You can't be thinking about too many things. Relief pitchers have to get into a zone of their own. I just hope I'm stupid enough.

Dan Quisenberry

Forget about the funny things he said through the course of his career and the side-winding, submarine, slingshot fling of a pitch he threw. The Quiz was outstanding, one of the best relief aces the game has ever seen. In a six-year period (1980-85), no one in the AL was better.

Dan used his slider and an incredible penchant for control to befuddle American League hitters during his career. A workhorse for the Royals pitching staff, Dan threw more than 125 innings for the club five different times. His presence in the bullpen is what finally pushed the team over the top and into the World Series in 1980. And when the pitching staff fell on hard times in 1983, he held it together, garnering a Major League record number of saves.

Despite his pitching talents, Dan might best be remembered for his wit, quotes, outlook on life and love of the game of baseball. He was always fast to remind fans that he knew how lucky he was to be a baseball player. Royals' fans knew they were lucky he played in Kansas City, and with his tragic passing at the end of the 1998 season, the Royals, Kansas City and all of baseball lost one of the truly great men to grace the playing fields of the Major Leagues.

1. When did Quiz appear in his first Royals game?

2. When did he earn his first save?

3. How many times did Quiz lead the AL in saves?

4. By the end of the 1984 season, Dan accomplished something that had never been done in the majors before. What did he do?

5. How many different colleges did Quiz attend, and what are their names?

6. How many All-Star games was Quiz selected for?

7. Did Dan ever start a game in the Majors?

8. Quiz pitched for two other teams at the end of his career. Who were they?

9. How many games did Quiz appear in for the Royals?

10. How many times did he lead the American League in games pitched?

Dan Quisenberry

Steve Busby

Steve Busby

Steve Busby ripped through the American League his first two seasons with the Royals. He won 40 games, tossed two no-hitters, and as if there was any doubt to his pitching ability, set an American League record by putting down 33 consecutive batters in one stretch. No question, he was the Royals' first great pitcher. And it is no stretch to say Cooperstown was in his future.

A rotator cuff injury basically ended his career—1975 was the last time he started more than 30 games—and while he dabbled with the club on and off through 1980, Busby was pitching more from memory and guile than physical talent. He won three games in 1976, missed all of the 1977 season, and won another eight games before quitting for good after the 1980 season.

Steve left his mark on the club and Major League Baseball during his short stint, and established many team records with his competitive, tough spirit and pitching prowess. Imagine: what if the Royals had had a healthy Steve Busby throughout the late '70s and '80s?

1. What university did Steve attend?

2. When did Steve make his debut with the Royals?

3. How many All-Star games was Steve selected for?

4. How many times was Busby the opening day pitcher for the Royals?

5. What award did Steve win in 1973?

6. Steve did something special in just his 10th Major League start. What was it?

7. When and where did he throw his two no-hitters?

8. How many games did he win for the Royals in his career?

9. What other Major League teams did Steve pitch for?

10. What was Steve's career high for strikeouts in a game?

Dennis Leonard

Dennis pitched two no-hitters in the minors, tossed countless big-game wins for the Royals, and was considered the team's money pitcher for most of his career. He was also the Majors' winningest right-handed pitcher from 1975-81, chalking up 130 victories in that time span. Yet he might best be remembered for his return to the Royals after nearly three years on the disabled list and four knee operations; Dennis pitched a dramatic 1-0 complete game win over the Blue Jays at Royals Stadium on April 12, 1986. That one game, maybe more than any other in his terrific career, showed his determination, will and ability, and why he was a great pitcher.

Dennis won the Royals Pitcher of the Year Award three times, and holds the club record for complete games, strikeouts and shutouts. He faced his hardest luck in the ALCS, losing three times to the Yankees. But he also won the important second game of the 1980 ALCS, a win that led to the Royals' sweep of the Yankees that year.

1. How did the Royals acquire Dennis?

2. Where did Dennis go to high school?

3. Dennis was an all-conference selection in college. Where did he go?

4. When did Dennis make his Major League debut?

5. Dennis Leonard won 144 games for the Royals in 12 seasons. How many times did he win 20 or more games?

6. How many games did he lose in his career?

7. In 1979 Dennis led the AL in one pitching category. What was it?

8. Dennis tied for the American League lead in wins once. What year did he accomplish this?

9. Dennis led the American League in one other pitching category in 1981. What was the category, and the number posted by Dennis?

10. Dennis led the American League in games started three times. What three years did he lead?

Dennis Leonard

Cookie Rojas

Born in Havana, Cuba, on March 6, 1939, Cookie was one of the first stars to play in Kansas City, bringing several skills to the field of play when he joined the Royals in 1970. He teamed with Fred Patek to give KC a talented keystone combo, and was instrumental in the team's rise to the top of the AL West. Voted the American League's top second baseman in 1971, Cookie led the junior circuit in fielding percentage that season with a .991 mark.

An all-time favorite of the Kansas City fans, Cookie made a comfortable shift into a utility role after Frank White took over second base, and still made winning contributions to the team through the 1977 season. He finished his career with 1,660 hits, a .263 batting average, and led the American League in fielding percentage twice.

1. What team did Cookie begin his career with?
2. What pitcher did Cookie collect his first Major League hit off of?
3. How many times was Cookie selected for the All-Star team as a Royal?
4. He was selected once for the National League. What team was he playing for, and in what year did he represent them?
5. How many hits did Rojas have in All-Star competition?
6. How many times in his career did Cookie hit .300 or better?
7. How did the Royals acquire Cookie?
8. Who was the second baseman Cookie replaced in the lineup?
9. In 1988, Cookie took on the managerial duties of what team?

Cookie Rojas

Fred Patek

How short it too short? Fred Patek held the distinction of being the shortest player in the Major Leagues throughout his career. He proved, however, that good things come in small packages. After joining Kansas City in 1971, the slick-fielding shortstop quickly established himself as a catalyst at the plate and in the field. Patek's prowess for stealing bases helped the Royals score runs. In the field, he led AL shortstops in double plays four consecutive seasons, 1971-74.

A hitter when it counted most, Patek batted .389 in both the 1976 and 1977 ALCS. He hit a home run in the Royals' only win of the 1978 ALCS. With the exception of home runs and batting average, Patek remains in the top ten of almost all of the Royals' career batting records. Patek was always a fan favorite, and played 1,245 games for the Royals.

1. The Royals acquired Freddie Patek in a six-player deal with what team?

2. What two players came to the Royals with Patek?

3. How tall is Freddie?

4. How many times did Patek lead the American League in stolen bases?

5. True or False: Patek led the league in triples three times.

6. How many All-Star games was Patek selected for?

7. What team did Patek finish his career with?

8. Patek hit for the cycle in 1971 off what Minnesota pitcher?

9. How many lifetime stolen bases does Patek have?

10. What was Patek's lifetime batting average?

Fred Patek

John Mayberry

John Mayberry

A Detroit native, Big John came to the Royals in one of the club's best trades and immediately became the big hitter on the team. He swatted 25 homers and knocked in 100 runs in his first season with Kansas City, and continued to produce top offensive numbers throughout his stay with the Royals. His best season was 1975, when he crashed 34 home runs, batted .291 and collected 106 RBIs. Always extremely agile around first base, John was considered one of the best fielding first basemen in the American League. Twice he led the league in fielding percentage.

Mayberry's numbers dropped dramatically in 1976 (.232 BA, 13 HR), and while he rebounded a bit and hit 23 home runs in 1977, his batting average was again low at .230. Big John was traded to Toronto before the start of the 1978 season.

Despite his relatively short stay in Kansas City, Mayberry remains a fan favorite, and is still in the top 10 of many of the club's offensive records.

1. What team traded Mayberry to the Royals, and who else was involved in the trade?

2. John led the American League in this category twice, in 1973 and again in 1975. What's the category, and how many?

3. How many times was Mayberry selected for the All-Star team?

4. How many home runs did Mayberry hit as a Royal?

5. How many home runs did Mayberry hit in the 1976 ALCS?

6. How many times in his career did John hit three home runs in a game?

7. Mayberry led the American League in on-base percentage once. What year did he do it, and what was the percentage?

8. John finished second in the American League MVP voting in 1975. Who won the award that season?

9. What was Mayberry's lifetime batting average?

10. What team did he finish his career with?

Larry Gura

When Larry Gura joined the Royals in the middle of the 1976 season, it was impossible to know the kind of impact he was going to have on the future success of the team. From his pennant-saving performance against Oakland at the end of the '76 season to his brilliant pitching in the 1980 World Series, Larry provided outstanding left-handed stuff on the Royals' staff for more than nine seasons. That he ended his career as fourth in all-time wins on the club with 111 is not only a tribute to his effectiveness as a pitcher, but also his ability just to win games.

1. Larry was an All-American pitcher at what university?

2. What team did Larry defeat twice in the College World Series to help lead his school to the national title?

3. What two Major League teams did Gura play for before joining the Royals?

4. Who did the Royals trade to acquire Larry?

5. What was Gura's highest win total in one season?

6. What team did he finish his career with?

7. How many games did Gura win in the 1980 World Series?

8. How many All-Star games was he selected for?

9. What was Gura's ERA for the 1980 World Series?

10. Larry posted a career high for saves with 10 in 1977. What was his second-highest season total after that?

Larry Gura

Jeff Montgomery

The Royals' all-time leader in saves, Jeff fell into the closer role much as Dan Quisenberry had a decade earlier and quickly established himself as one of the best in the Majors. He became Kansas City's closer by the process of elimination, but he also came very close to never getting the opportunity to show the Royals what he could do.

On the verge of being sent to the minors during spring training in 1989, it was suggested to Jeff by one of his coaches that he simply throw the ball over the plate—and so he did. His use of four different pitches in closing situations was a bit of a deviation from the normal closer, but it proved to be his strongest point. After his initial success, Montgomery rewrote the Royals relief pitching statistics and records, appearing in 686 games for Kansas City.

1. What university did Jeff attend?

2. When and how did the Royals acquire Jeff?

3. When did Jeff appear in his first game for the Royals?

4. How many career starts does Jeff have?

5. When did Montgomery record his first Major League save?

6. Jeff won one Rolaids Relief Man award. What year did he win?

7. How many All-Star games has Jeff been selected for?

8. How many career saves does Jeff have?

9. How many career wins does Jeff have?

Jeff Montgomery

Kevin Appier

Kevin Appier took his place among the other great Royals' pitchers in 1997 by posting his 100th win for the club. The combative Lancaster, California, native became the ace of the Royals staff in 1995, and was one of the top pitchers in the American League for almost a decade. Appier's long-reaching, hard deliveries were a staple around the American League, and his slider was considered the best in the league for a righthander. While his win totals didn't always measure up among the top pitchers in the league, his other numbers did. He consistently posted low ERAs, his best coming in 1992 at 2.46. His fiery, competitive nature was always evident on the mound.

Appier finished the 1997 season as the fifth winningest pitcher in the club's history with 111 wins, is seventh in career ERA, and fourth in career games started with 275, and 10th in complete games. Appier was traded during the 1999 season, but returned to Kansas City and finished his career with the Royals in 2004. He was inducted into the Royals Hall of Fame in 2011.

1. What two colleges did Appier attend?

2. How did the Royals acquire Kevin Appier?

3. When did he pitch in his first game for the Royals?

4. When did he win his first game for the Royals?

5. When did Appier win his 100th game?

6. How many times did Appier appear in the All-Star game?

7. Kevin won the American League ERA title in 1993. What was his ERA that season?

8. How many times was Appier the Opening Day pitcher for KC?

9. How many times in his career did Appier record 200 or more strikeouts in a season?

10. Kevin became the first Royal and 27th Major League pitcher to achieve a rare feat. What is it?

Paul Splittorff

The Royals all-time winningest pitcher, Splitt was the mainstay of the team's early pitching staffs, and an important member during the championship years in the late '70s. He logged more than 1,000 Ks in his career, and is Kansas City's all-time leader in games started with 392.

A clutch performer, Splitt always pitched well for the team in the playoffs, and it is still a puzzle to many fans why he didn't pitch more in the 1980 World Series. Following his career on the mound, he shared an insider's view of the game from the broadcast booth at Kauffman Stadium, enlightening viewers and listeners with his baseball expertise.

Splittorff died on May 25, 2011, from complications caused by oral cancer and melanoma.

1. What college did Splitt attend?

2. When did Paul make his first appearance for the Royals?

3. When did Paul pick up his first win for the Royals?

4. Paul was the first Royal to win 20 games in a season. What season did he accomplish this?

5. Paul won more games than any other pitcher in Royals' history. How many wins does he have?

6. Paul also has the distinction of losing more games than any other Royals' pitcher. How many times did he lose in his career?

7. How many career strikeouts does Paul have?

8. Paul appeared in four different ALCS. What is his overall won-lost record for the ALCS?

9. Splitt never threw a no-hitter, but came close several times. How many one-hitters did he pitch?

10. Paul did color commentary for both the Royals radio and TV networks. True or false?

Alex Gordon

As the Royals' second overall pick in the 2005 draft, Alex Gordon came into the organization as one of the most highly-touted prospects in the franchise's history. He had won almost every award possible during his final season in college, and was as close to a "can't miss" player that the Royals had ever drafted.

But he did miss. Gordon hit just .247 his rookie season, and followed that with a .260 hitting performance. His third year was even worse, and the Royals sent him back to the minors.

But Gordon wasn't finished, and he proceeded to re-invent himself.

With the help of hitting coach Kevin Seitzer, Gordon changed his hitting style, and also changed positions, moving to the outfield. The effect was dramatic. Gordon hit .303 in 2011, socked 23 homers, and knocked in 87 runs. He also won a Gold Glove for his fielding prowess in the outfield. His hitting stayed strong the next couple of seasons, and he won the Gold Glove again.

"It means a lot," Gordon said of his Gold Glove in 2013. "The first one was pretty special, just because it's the first one, but to be able to share it with two teammates (Hosmer and Perez) makes this one the best one of all."

1. What positions has Gordon played for the Royals?

2. Where did Gordon attend high school?

3. Where did Gordon play collegiate baseball?

4. What was the outcome of his first major league at bat?

5. How many Gold Gloves has Gordon won?

6. What was the baseball card snafu that happened in 2006 with his baseball card?

7. What year was he selected for the MLB All Star game?

8. With what team did Gordon start the 2010 season?

9. Gordon lead all major league outfielders in what stat in 2011?

10. What batting stat did Gordon lead the majors in 2012?

Alex Gordon

Billy Butler

Billy Butler

The man loves to hit, and throughout his career in Kansas City, he produced big hit after big hit for the Royals. While he has played a little bit of first base, Billy Butler has become the best designated hitter for the Royals since Hal McRae. Butler won the 2012 Edgar Martinez Outstanding Designated Hitter Award, just the second Royals DH to win the honor. Hal McRae was the top DH in 1976, '80 and '82.

"He's just really starting to come into his own as a force in the American League offensively," Royals manager Ned Yost said of Butler winning the award. "As proud as I was of him last year, just for the production that he brought forth, I think he's going to continue to get better and better and produce more and more."

1. When did Butler make his major league debut?

2. What was the result of Butler's first major league at bat?

3. Where did Butler receive a scholarship to play college baseball and did he choose to attend?

4. What is Butler's legal name?

5. Why did Butler receive the Hutch Award in 2011, an award for players that exemplifies honor, courage and dedication both on and off the field?

6. What three MLB honors did Butler receive in 2012?

7. What honor did Butler receive from playing in the 2006 All-Star Futures game?

8. Where did Butler play his rookie season?

9. What high school did Butler graduate from?

10. What round was Butler drafted in and by whom?

11. What nickname did the fans begin calling Butler in the summer of 2011?

Mark Gubicza

Of all the strong, young arms the Royals had on their staff in the early 1980s, it seemed that if any one of them was expendable, it would be Mark Gubicza. Yet one by one the Royals dismantled the staff; first Danny Jackson, then Charlie Leibrandt and Bret Saberhagen. Through it all Gubicza remained, not leaving until after the 1996 season.

Gubicza left his mark on the Royals' record book. He is third on the all-time win list, second in career starts, innings pitched and career losses. Gubicza compiled steady, unspectacular numbers throughout his career in a Royals uniform, and maybe that was the secret that kept him in Kansas City. He never had a truly horrible season, except 1996, and always kept the team in the game.

His departure from Kansas City marked the end of an era; he was the last of the 1985 world champs that was still with the club.

1. Where did Mark go to high school?

2. When did Mark pitch in his first game for the Royals? Against what team?

3. When did Mark earn his first Major League victory?

4. How many career wins for the Royals does Mark have?

5. How many All-Star games was Gubicza selected for?

6. How many games of the 1985 World Series did Mark pitch in?

7. What season did Mark win 20 games?

8. Mark holds the club record for strikeouts in a game. How many, and against what team did he set the record?

9. In 1988 Mark finished third in the AL Cy Young award voting. What two pitchers finished ahead of him?

Mike Sweeney

Making it to the big leagues was never a sure thing for Mike Sweeney. Selected by the Royals in the 10th round of the 1991 draft, Sweeney was almost traded a couple of times because the club didn't think he would fit into their plans. But he was too good of a hitter, and when he was switched to first base in 1999, his career took off.

In 2000, Sweeney showed that he was one of the best hitters in baseball—he hit .333 with 29 home runs and a club record of 144 RBIs. He was also selected to play in his first All-Star game.

Hampered by back problems the last half of his career, Sweeney still hit .297 with 215 home runs and 909 RBIs for his career. And while his best seasons for the Royals happened to be when the team was at its worst, Sweeney had no regrets.

"I know I've been blessed like very few people have ever been blessed," Sweeney said of his time in Kansas City. "I've loved every minute of it."

1. When did Sweeney hit his first major league home run?

2. What statistic did Sweeney and Carlos Delgado tie for the lead in the AL in 2000?

3. What was Sweeney's career-high RBI count in a single game?

4. What was Sweeney's first major league hit?

5. How many major league teams did Sweeney play on?

6. At what position was Mike drafted to start his baseball career?

7. How many All-Star games was Sweeney selected for?

8. What years did Mike serve as team captain for the Royals?

9. Was Sweeney drafted out of high school or college, and what school did he attend?

10. What happened to delay the game each time Mike came to bat on his last game with the Royals, September 30, 2007?

Carlos Beltran

In a different era of baseball, Carlos Beltran would have played the majority of his career with the Royals. But even though he was with the Royals for just over five seasons, he is still be considered one of the greatest players ever to roam the field at Kauffman Stadium.

Selected in second round of the June 1995 draft, it was apparent from the start that Beltran was going to be a special player. He flew through the Royals' minor league system, and by 1999 made a place for himself on the team's roster. His rookie season was fantastic (22 HRs, 108 RBI, and 27 stolen bases), and Beltran was named the AL Rookie of the Year. Over the next four seasons he played at an amazingly high level.

"Carlos is the most gifted baseball player I've ever seen," Johnny Damon said of his teammate. Beltran could do it all: hit for power, steal bases, and play great defense. He hit 29 homers in 2002, and in 2003 stole 41 bases.

"Carlos Beltran is the type of player who comes around once in a decade," Mike Sweeney said.

On June 24, 2004, the Royals traded Beltran to the Houston Astros.

1. What country is Carlos from?

2. What year did he make his major league debut?

3. Beltran played for Omaha briefly in the year 2000. What was the name of the team that season?

4. How many Gold Gloves did Beltran win while playing for the Royals?

5. How many All Star games did he play in while with the Royals?

6. How many times did he knock in at least 100 runs for the Royals?

7. Beltran easily won the 1999 Rookie of the Year award. Who finished a distant second that year?

8. In 2003, the Royals finished with a winning record: 83-79. How many home runs did he hit that season?

Royal Numbers

Career Leaders
Batting

Games Played

2,707	George Brett
2,324	Frank White
1,891	Amos Otis
1,837	Hal McRae
1,787	Willie Wilson
1,282	Mike Sweeney

At-bats

10,349	George Brett
7,859	Frank White
7,050	Amos Otis
6,799	Willie Wilson
6,568	Hal McRae

Runs

1,583	George Brett
1,074	Amos Otis
1,060	Willie Wilson
912	Frank White
873	Hal McRae

Hits

3,154	George Brett
2,006	Frank White
1,977	Amos Otis
1,968	Willie Wilson
1,924	Hal McRae

Doubles

665	George Brett
449	Hal McRae
407	Frank White
365	Amos Otis
297	Mike Sweeney

Triples

137	George Brett
133	Willie Wilson
65	Amos Otis
63	Hal McRae

Home Runs

317	George Brett
197	Mike Sweeney
193	Amos Otis
169	Hal McRae
160	Frank White
142	John Mayberry

Runs Batted In

1,595	George Brett
1,012	Hal McRae
992	Amos Otis
886	Frank White
837	Mike Sweeney

Batting Average
(minimum 500 games)

.306	Jose Offerman
.305	George Brett
.299	Mike Sweeney
.298	Billy Butler
.294	Kevin Seitzer

Stolen Bases

612	Willie Wilson
340	Amos Otis
336	Fred Patek
201	George Brett
178	Frank White

Pitching

Earned-Run Average
(minimum 500 innings)

2.55	Dan Quisenberry
3.05	Steve Farr
3.05	Steve Mingori
3.08	Roger Nelson
3.20	Jeff Montgomery
3.21	Bret Saberhagen

Wins

166	Paul Splittorff
144	Dennis Leonard
132	Mark Gubicza
115	Kevin Appier
111	Larry Gura
110	Bret Saberhagen

Losses

143	Paul Splittorff
135	Mark Gubicza
106	Dennis Leonard
92	Kevin Appier
78	Larry Gura

Innings Pitched

2,554.2	Paul Splittorff
2,218.2	Mark Gubicza
2,187.0	Dennis Leonard
1,843.2	Kevin Appier
1,701.1	Larry Gura

Strikeouts

1,458	Kevin Appier
1,366	Mark Gubicza
1,323	Dennis Leonard
1,093	Bret Saberhagen
1,057	Paul Splittorff

Bases on Balls

783	Mark Gubicza
780	Paul Splittorff
634	Kevin Appier
622	Dennis Leonard
587	Tom Gordon

Games

686	Jeff Montgomery
573	Dan Quisenberry
429	Paul Splittorff
382	Mark Gubicza
312	Dennis Leonard

Shutouts

23	Dennis Leonard
17	Paul Splittorff
16	Mark Gubicza
14	Larry Gura
14	Bret Saberhagen

Saves

304	Jeff Montgomery
238	Dan Quisenberry
160	Joakim Soria
67	Greg Holland
58	Doug Bird

Complete Games

103	Dennis Leonard
88	Paul Splittorff
64	Bret Saberhagen
61	Larry Gura
53	Steve Busby
53	Dick Drago

Winning Percentage

.593	Al Fitzmorris
.587	Larry Gura
	David Cone
.586	Steve Farr
.585	Bret Saberhagen

Single Season Records
Batting

At-bats 705	Willie Wilson	1980
Runs 136	Johnny Damon	20o0
Singles 184	Willie Wilson	1980
Doubles 54	Hal McRae	1977
Triples 21	Willie Wilson	1985
Home Runs 36	Steve Balboni	1985
Grand Slams 3	Danny Tartabull	1988
	Yuniesky Betancourt	2010
RBIs 144	Mike Sweeney	2000
Walks 122	John Mayberry	1973
Batting Average 390	George Brett	1980
Slugging Pct 664	George Brett	1980
Stolen Bases 83	Willie Wilson	1979

Pitching

Games 84	Dan Quisenberry	1985
Complete Games 21	Dennis Leonard	1977
Innings 294.2	Dennis Leonard	1978
Wins 23	Bret Saberhagen	1989
Losses 19	Paul Splittorff	1974
	Darrell May	2004
Winning Pct. 793	Bret Saberhagen	1989
Walks 120	Mark Gubicza	1987
Strikeouts 244	Dennis Leonard	1977
Shutouts 6	Roger Nelson	1972
Home runs allowed 38	Darrell May	2004
Lowest ERA 2.08	Roger Nelson	1972
Saves 47	Greg Holland	2013

Year-by-Year Results

Year	Position	Won	Lost	Pct.	GB
1969	Fourth	69	93	.426	28
1970	Fourth(Tied)	65	97	.401	33
1971	Second	85	76	.528	16
1972	Fourth	76	78	.494	16.5
1973	Second	88	74	.543	6
1974	Fifth	77	85	.475	13
1975	Second	91	71	.562	7
1976	First	90	72	.556	+2.5
1977	First	102	60	.630	+8
1978	First	92	70	.567	+5
1979	Second	85	77	.525	3
1980	First	97	65	.599	+14
1981	Fourth	50	53	.485	11
1982	Second	90	72	.556	3
1983	Second	79	83	.488	20
1984	First	84	78	.519	+3
1985	First	91	71	.562	+1
1986	Third (Tied)	76	86	.469	16
1987	Second	83	79	.512	2
1988	Third	84	77	.522	19.5
1989	Second	92	70	.568	7
1990	Sixth	75	86	.466	27.5
1991	Sixth	82	80	.506	13
1992	Fifth (Tied)	72	90	.444	24
1993	Third	84	78	.519	10
1994	Third	64	51	.557	4
1995	Second	70	74	.486	30
1996	Fifth	75	86	.466	24
1997	Fifth	67	93	.419	19
1998	Third	72	89	.447	16.5
1999	Fourth	64	97	.398	32.5
2000	Fourth	77	85	.475	18.0
2001	Fifth	65	97	.401	26.0
2002	Fourth	62	100	.383	32.5
2003	Third	83	79	.512	7.0
2004	Fifth	58	104	.358	34.0
2005	Fifth	56	106	.346	43.0
2006	Fifth	62	100	.383	34.0
2007	Fifth	69	93	.426	27.0
2008	Fourth	75	87	.463	13.5
2009	Fourth	65	97	.401	21.5
2010	Fifth	67	95	.414	27.0
2011	Fourth	71	91	.438	24.0
2012	Third	72	90	.444	16.0
2013	Third	86	76	.531	7.0

Mark Stallard

Royals Hall of Fame
Listed by Year of Induction

1986
Steve Busby, SP
Amos Otis, CF

1987
Dick Howser, Manager
Cookie Rojas, 2B
Paul Splittorff, SP

1989
Dennis Leonard, SP
Hal McRae, DH

1992
Joe Burke, GM and President
Larry Gura, SP
Freddie Patek, SS

1993
Ewing Kauffman, owner

1994
George Brett, 3B

1995
Frank White, 2B

1996
Muriel Kauffman, executive
and wife of Ewing
John Mayberry, 1B

1998
Dan Quisenberry, RP

2000
Whitey Herzog, Manager
Willie Wilson, CF

2003
Jeff Montgomery, RP

2004
Denny Matthews, radio announcer

2005
Bret Saberhagen, SP

2006
Mark Gubicza, SP

2008
Art Stewart, scout

2011
Kevin Appier, SP

2012
George Toma, grounds keeper

More
Trivia

Ewing Kauffman

Ewing Kauffman

When Kansas City needed someone to step up and take control of the city's baseball fortunes, Ewing Kauffman took over and hit a grand slam. Through his guidance, leadership, integrity and strong ownership, the Royals achieved overwhelming success. Mr. K wanted to give Kansas City a winning baseball team, and he delivered. The Royals became one of the top franchises in the Major Leagues, winning six division titles, two American League pennants and a World Series championship during his tenure as the club's top man.

1. When did Ewing Kauffman purchase the team that was to become the Royals?

2. Where was Mr. Kauffman born?

3. What branch of the Armed Services did Mr. K serve in?

4. What year did Mr. K start the pharmaceutical firm that later became Marion Labs?

5. In what year did the Kansas City Press Club vote Mr. K their Man-of-the-Year?

6. What date was the Royals Stadium name changed to Kauffman Stadium?

7. Who was in charge of the Royals for seven years following Kauffman's death?

Mark Gubicza

Pitchers

1. This pitcher set the club record for the most wins by a rookie pitcher. Who is he?

2. Who is the only three-time 20-game winner in Royals' history?

3. When this pitcher made his first start for the Royals, he was the youngest pitcher ever to start a game for the Royals. Who is he, and how old was he?

4. Only one pitcher in Royals' history has ever struck out four batters in an inning. Who is the pitcher?

5. The highest win total in a season by a Royals' pitcher is 23. Who holds this record?

6. This pitcher holds the club record for the most consecutive wins during a season. Who is he, how many did he win in a row, and what year did he accomplish the mark?

7. Who was the Royals' first 20-game winner, and what season did he post the 20 wins?

8. This pitcher twice posted the lowest ERA on the Royals, first in 1974, and again in 1976. Who is he?

9. The club record for complete games is 21, set in 1977. Who set the mark?

10. This pitcher held the Royals' record for saves in a season, 23, until Quisenberry broke it in 1980 with 33. Who had this record?

11. The most starts ever by a KC pitcher was done in 1978. Who did it, and how many?

12. Only three pitchers in club history have ever posted 200-strikeout seasons. Who are they, and when did they top the 200 K mark?

13. Has any Royals' pitcher ever pitched 300 innings in a single season?

14. Who holds the club record for the lowest ERA in a season (starters)?

15. Who holds the Royals' record for the most losses in a season?

16. This pitcher tossed 6 shutouts for Kansas City in 1972, still the top mark in club history. Who is he?

17. Three pitchers have lost more than 100 games in Royals' history. Who are they, and how many games did each lose?

18. This pitcher has been the Royals' Opening Day starter more than anyone else, taking the mound 6 times to start the season. Who is he?

19. Only one pitcher has ever won a Gold Glove Award for the Royals. Who is he, and what year did he win the award?

20. Who was the Royals' first (1969) Opening Day pitcher?

21. Three different pitchers have won the Cy Young Award while playing for the Royals. Who are they, and when did they win the award?

22. This pitcher won the Cy Young Award in the National League and signed as a free agent with the Royals the following season. Who is he?

23. This Hall-of-Famer won more than 300 games and finished his career with Kansas City. Who is he, and what year did he pitch for the Royals?

24. This pitcher led the Royals in saves in 1978 and 1979. Who is he?

25. The pitcher holds the Royals' club record of 18 starts in a row without a loss. Who is he?

26. Four pitchers have recorded more than 40 saves in a season for the Royals. Who are they?

27. This pitcher was the Royals' lone All-Star selection in 1997 and 1999. Who is he?

28. This pitcher tied Paul Splittorff for the most losses in a season with 19 in 2004. Who is he?

29. Who owns the single-game strikeout record for the Royals?

30. The Royals' record for the most innings pitched in a game is 13. Who holds the record, and what season did he do it?

Catchers

1. Darrell Porter joined the Royals in December 1976, but was not the Opening Day catcher at the start of the 1977 season. Who was?

2. Jim Sundberg spent the majority of his career with the Texas Rangers, but what team did he come to the Royals from?

3. Who was the first Royals catcher to win a Gold Glove Award, and in what year did he win the award?

4. Who was the Royals' Opening Day catcher in 1980?

5. Who was the Royals' Opening Day catcher in 1969?

6. Who holds the Royals' season record for the most RBIs by a catcher?

7. Mike MacFarlane left Kansas City for one season, 1995, and returned for the 1996 season. What team did he play with in 1995?

8. This catcher was the Royals' top draft pick in 1989. He played with Kansas City from 1990 through 1995, and then went to the Mets. Who is he?

9. This catcher had his best seasons with the Royals, but won the World Series MVP with a National League team. Who is he?

10. Who was the Royals' Opening Day catcher in 1987?

11. The Royals' opening day catcher from 1974-76, this backstop was traded to the Yankees for Larry Gura on May 16, 1976. Who is he?

12. The Royals used four different catchers during the 2000 season. Name one of them.

Jamie Quirk

13. This catcher came to the Royals in the Carlos Beltran trade and caught more than 500 games for Kansas City. Who is he?

14. What team did Darrell Porter finish his career with?

15. This catcher hit a career-high 23 home runs for the Royals in 2009. Who is he?

16. This catcher came to the Royals at the end of his career and played in 118 games in 2010. Who is he?

17. Salvador Perez made his major league debut in 2011. How many hits did he get in his first game?

Darrell Porter

First Basemen

1. Who was the Royals' Opening Day first baseman in 1969?

2. His first team was the Yankees, and he returned there after leaving KC. He also played for Seattle and Texas. Who is he?

3. Willie Aikens came to KC in 1980 from what American League team?

4. This Royal started at first in 1971 after opening in the outfield in 1969 and at third base in 1970. Who is he?

5. This Royal played 92 consecutive games at first base between 1976 and 1979 without committing an error. Who is he?

6. A highly publicized rookie, this Royal took over first base at the start of the 1978 season. Who is he?

7. Wally Joyner came to Kansas City from California as a free agent before the 1992 season. What team was he traded to after the 1995 season?

8. Steve Balboni was the main first baseman from 1984-86, and also a little in 1987. Who was the first baseman in 1983?

9. John Mayberry debuted for the Royals in 1972. What team did Kansas City acquire him from?

10. Who started at first base in 1996's Opening Day game?

11. This player filled in at first and played an important backup role for the Royals from 1977 through 1980. He came to KC from the Chicago Cubs. Who is he?

12. He was the Opening Day starter at first base in 1987, but started at third from 1988 through 1991. Who is he?

13. John Mayberry was traded to what team before the start of the 1978 season?

14. Four Royals' first basemen have been selected for the All-Star game. Who are they?

15. Who was the Royals' main first baseman in 2007 and 2008?

Second Basemen

1. Who was the Royals' opening day second baseman in 1969?

2. Luis Alcaraz started the 1970 season at second. Who took his place in June?

3. How many consecutive seasons was Frank White the opening day second baseman?

4. Who replaced Frank White in the starting lineup at the beginning of the 1991 season?

5. He was one of the Royals' top utility players in 1976, appearing in 46 games at second base and 22 at DH. He also stole 15 bases that season. Who is he?

6. He played 61 games at second base in 1994, 84 games in 1996. He was traded just before the start of the 1997 season to Atlanta. Who is he?

7. Bobby Knoop filled in at second base for Kansas City, appearing in 52 games in 1971 and 33 in 1972. What two teams did he play for before coming to KC?

8. This versatile utility player was the Royals' second baseman in 93 games during the 1992 season, but played there only three more times through the 1995 season. Who is he?

9. A fixture in the Royals' infield in the late '70s and early '80s, this player was the club's main shortstop for five years. But he also appeared in more than 100 games at second base during his career. Who is he?

10. Only one other second baseman besides Frank White has won a Gold Glove. Who is he, and what year did he win?

11. The Royals used seven second basemen during the 2004 season. Name one of them.

12. Who was the Royals' main second baseman from 1999 to 2002?

13. This player came up through the Royals' farm system and was the main second baseman in 2010. Who is he?

14. Who was the Royals' Opening Day second baseman in 2013?

Third Basemen

1. Who was the Royals' starting third baseman in 1969?

2. Who played third most of the time in 1970?

3. Who was the Royals' opening day starting third baseman from 1971 through 1974?

4. When did George Brett become the regular third baseman?

5. After starting at first base, this rookie took over third, with Brett moving to first. Who is he?

6. While Brett was on the DL during the 1984 season, this utility man played a key role in the Royals' drive to the AL West title with his fielding and hitting. Who is he?

7. After productive seasons in Minnesota and California, this third sacker's best years appeared to be behind him when he signed with KC in 1993. Who is he?

8. Who holds the Royals' record for the most home runs hit by a third baseman?

9. What team did the Royals acquire Dean Palmer from?

10. How many Gold Glove awards have Kansas City third basemen won?

11. The Royals traded Joe Randa to the Pittsburgh Pirates after the 1996 season. The Arizona Diamondbacks selected him in the expansion draft prior to the 1998 season and then traded him. What team did Randa play for in 1998?

12. Who became the Royals' everyday third baseman in 2005?

13. Who took over at third base for Alex Gordon in 2009?

14. Who became the Royals everyday third baseman in 2011?

Paul Schaal

Shortstops

1. Who was the Royals' Opening Day shortstop in 1969?

2. How many times was Fred Patek the Royals' starting shortstop on opening day?

3. Who replaced Fred Patek as the Royals' shortstop in the starting lineup?

4. The Royals primarily used two shortstops in 1985. Who are they?

5. Who was the Opening Day shortstop in 1986?

6. Who did the Royals trade to acquire Kurt Stillwell?

7. This shortstop was with the Royals from 1970 through 1974 and was in the starting lineup on Opening Day in 1972. Who is he?

8. The Royals signed this shortstop away from division rival Minnesota, and he was their starting shortstop from 1993 through 1995. Who is he?

9. This player, while primarily a shortstop, has also played second and third base, as well as the outfield, for Kansas City. But in 1992, he was the Opening Day shortstop. Who is he?

10. What teams did U.L. Washington play for after he left the Royals?

11. This infielder played 29 games at shortstop for the Royals in 1974, 42 in 1975, and 37 in 1976. Who is he?

12. Who was the backup shortstop when the Royals won the American League in 1980?

13. The Royals used three different shortstops in 1970. Who were they?

14. This infielder played at least one game at shortstop every year from 1974 through 1978. Who is he?

15. How many Gold Gloves have Kansas City shortstops won?

16. This shortstop won the 2003 American League Rookie of the Year Award. Who is he?

17. What team did Alcides Escobar play for before the Royals?

U. L. Washington

Outfielders

1. What three players made up the Royals' Opening Day outfield in 1969?

2. Lou Piniella won the 1969 American League Rookie of the Year award. What team did the Royals acquire him from?

3. After a long, productive career with the Reds, this outfielder played for St. Louis, Cleveland and California before finishing up in Kansas City in 1974-75. Who is he?

4. After Piniella was traded, who initially took his spot in the outfield?

5. This outfielder finished second in the American League MVP voting for the 1977 season, then never received another MVP vote the rest of his career. Who is he?

6. This outfielder hit .302 and .292 in '76 and '77, then played for Boston and Texas before returning to the Royals in 1982 to end his career. Who is he?

7. How many different outfielders have won a Gold Glove while playing for Kansas City?

8. This outfielder was in the Royals 'starting lineup on Opening Day, 1977, but was out of baseball after the 1979 season. Who is he?

9. He played several positions, but was primarily an outfielder who was in the Royals' starting lineup at the beginning of the 1978, 1979, 1980 and 1981 seasons. He finished his career playing with the Reds, Mets and Cardinals. Who is he?

10. The Royals traded John Morris to the Cardinals for this left fielder in 1985. Who is he?

Pat Sheridan

11. Who did the Royals trade to Seattle to acquire Danny Tartabull?

12. Kansas City traded Rich Gale and Bill Laskey to the Giants for this outfielder, who played with the Royals in 1982-83. Who is he?

13. Hal McRae is one of two Royals to have played in 162 games in one season, and he did so in 1977. This outfielder is the other Royal to play in 162 games, and he also did it in 1977. Who is he?

15. A prolific base-stealer in the National League, this outfielder played two seasons in Kansas City, accumulating 50 stolen bases in his one full season before being traded. Who is he?

Jim Eisenreich

16. This outfielder hit two homes in the 1985 ALCS. He played for the Tigers, Giants, and Yankees after leaving the Royals. Who is he?

17. This outfielder was a starter in the 2000 All-Star Game. Who is he?

18. These outfielders led the league in assists in 2011 and 2012. Who are they?

19. This outfielder is the only other Royal besides Willie Wilson to lead the league in runs scored. Who is he?

20. This outfielder was hit by a pitch 23 times in 2007, which led the league. Who is he?

21. This Royal was the first outfielder selected for the All-Star game since 2000. Who is he?

Designated Hitters

1. Who was the Royals' first designated hitter?

2. How many different DH's did Kansas City use in 1973, the first year of the rule?

3. Who was the Royals' DH on Opening Day, 1975?

4. Who was the DH on Opening Day, 1976?

5. Who was the DH on Opening Day, 1985?

6. What position did Hal McRae play before settling into the DH spot in the lineup?

7. How many times was Hal McRae selected the American League Designated Hitter of the Year?

8. Before finishing his career as a DH, what position did George Brett play?

Ed Kirkpatrick

9. This former National League MVP was the Royals' designated hitter for 26 games in 1974. Who is he?

10. This future Royal was the Phillies' primary DH in the 1980 World Series. Who is he?

11. In 2009, Billy Butler played 145 games at first base. Who was the Royals' primary DH that season?

12. In 2010, this right-handed outfielder was used primarily as a DH. Who is he?

13. Billy Butler became a full-time DH in 2011. Who took over at first base?

Managers

1. Through the 2013 season, how many full-time managers have the Royals had?

2. Who was the Royals' first manager?

3. This manager was a long-time coach under Earl Weaver of the Orioles before taking control of the Royals. Who is he?

4. Bob Lemon took over when this manager was fired 42 games into the 1970 season. Who is he?

5. How many former Royals' players have managed the team, and who are they?

6. Which manager led the Royals to a first-place finish the second half of the 1981 season?

7. Which manager has served the longest?

8. Before becoming the Royals' manager in 2008, what team did Trey Hillman manage?

9. Which Royals' manager has the highest winning percentage (not counting interim managers)?

10. Who lost the most games?

11. Three different managers led the Royals to American League West Division Championships. Who are they?

12. How many games did the Royals win after Tony Muser became manager in 1997?

13. Only two managers have led the Royals to a winning record since 1994. Who are they?

14. When Dick Howser officially resigned because of his illness in 1987, who became the Royals' manager?

American League Championship Series

1976 ALCS
New York 3 games, Kansas City 2 games

*We've got the kind of club that's going to be good for a long time to come.
We're going to get better, but I don't think the Yankees are going to get better.*

Hal McRae
after the Royals lost the
1976 ALCS

The Royals went into the 1976 ALCS just happy to be playing for the pennant. This series will always be remembered for Chris Chambliss hitting the pennant-winning home run for New York, but the Royals also provided several exciting moments as well, particularly George Brett's game-tying homer the inning before Chambliss' shot.

The closeness of this series was a foreshadowing of things to come as these two rivals would become well acquainted in the playoffs throughout the rest of the decade.

John Mayberry tries to pick off the Yankees' Mickey Rivers during the '76 ALCS.

1. Two Royals hit home runs in this series. Who are they, and in what games did they homer?

2. Who started Game 1 for the Royals?

3. This pitcher started two games in the series, but didn't figure in either decision. Who is he?

4. This pitcher relieved Larry Gura in Game 4 and got the win. Who is he?

167

Fred Patek puts a tag on the Yankees Roy White in 1976 ALCS action.

5. Who had the highest batting average for the Royals in the series?

6. Amos Otis was hurt running to the bag in his first at bat of Game 1 and missed the rest of the series. Who replaced him in the outfield?

7. Who was on base when Brett hit his game-tying, three-run homer in Game 5?

8. Which Kansas City pitcher gave up the series-ending home run to the Yankees' Chris Chambliss?

9. How many bases did the Royals steal in the series?

1977 ALCS
New York 3 games, Kansas City 2 games

It looks like we can't get a World Series in this town.
Whitey Herzog
after 1977 ALCS

The heartbreak of 1976 was nothing compared to the devastating loss the Royals suffered in the 1977 ALCS. Up two games to one, Kansas City dropped the last two games at Royals Stadium, losing Game 5 in the 9th inning. The Yankees waltzed on to the World Series; the Royals added perhaps the hardest loss in the team's history to their legacy.

1. Who started and won Game 1 of the 1977 ALCS for the Royals?

2. Three Royals homered in Game 1. Who were they?

Fred Patek writhes in pain after being spiked by Reggie Jackson in Game 5 of the 1977 ALCS. Jackson, Frank White and George Brett look on. Patek continued to play in the game.

3. How many home runs did the Royals hit the rest of the series?

4. Who started Game 2 for the Royals?

5. Who started and pitched a complete game to win Game 3?

6. Who had three hits, including a double and triple, scored two runs and had an RBI in Game 4 for the Royals in a losing effort?

7. Who was the losing pitcher for the Royals in Game 5?

8. Who hit .444, the team high for KC in the series?

9. Who had an RBI pinch-hit single for the Yankees in the eighth inning to make the score 3-2 Royals?

10. Who made the last out for the Royals in Game 5, ending the series?

1978 ALCS
New York 3 games, Kansas City 1 game

Man, I want to beat these guys soooo bad!

Frank White
before the '78 series

Losing for the third year in a row was no easier than the first two times, but it didn't take as long. Kansas City might have played the Yankees tougher than in the two previous series, but could only win one time against the Bronx Bombers. George Brett hit three home runs in Game 3, and still the Yankees found a way to win. And as they did the year before, the Yankees went on to win the World Series.

New York's Thurman Munson pre-pares to leave the field after being thrown out in Game 2 action. Patek made the play as White looks on.

1. The Yankees had to win a one-game divisional playoff to qualify for the ALCS. Who did they beat to win the Eastern division?

2. The Royals won Game 2 of the series, 10-4. Who was the winning pitcher for Kansas City?

3. George Brett hit three home runs in Game 3 off the same pitcher. Who was the Yankee pitcher?

Pete LaCock hits in Game 2.

4. Who hit the game-winning home run for the Yankees in Game 3?

5. Who was the only other Royal to hit a home run in the series?

6. Which pitcher lost two of the three games for the Royals?

1980 ALCS
Kansas City 3 games, New York 0 games

Our fans think we've already won the World Series by beating the Yankees.

George Brett
after the Royals won
the '80 ALCS

Finally! After three futile tries against the Yankees, the Royals finally hit the jackpot and won the American League Championship Series. The Yankees did not go quietly though, as it took a dramatic three-run home run by George Brett in Game 3 to bring the AL pennant home to KC for the first time ever. Frank White also starred for the guys in blue, capturing the series MVP award.

1. Who started and won Game 1 of the series for Kansas City?

2. Who homered for Kansas City in Game 1?

George Brett receives congratulations from Lance Mulliniks after hitting a home run in Game 1 of the 1980 ALCS.

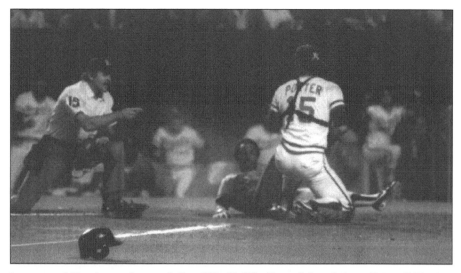

In one of the key plays of the '80 ALCS, Royals' catcher Darrell Porter looks back as Home Plate Umpire Ed Brinkman calls the Yankee runner out. George Brett made the peg that cut down what would have been the tying run.

3. Who pitched eight plus innings in Game 2, struck out eight batters and got the win for the Royals?

4. George Brett made a perfect peg to the plate to cut down the potential tying run in the top of the eighth inning of Game 2. Who was the Yankee runner he gunned down?

5. Frank White was the 1980 ALCS MVP. How many home runs did he hit in the series?

6. Who was the winning pitcher for the Royals in Game 3?

7. How many saves did Quiz have in the series?

Dennis Leonard, Jim Frey, George Brett, and Darrell Porter try to sort things out during Game 2.

8. Who was on base when Brett hit his pennant-winning home run in the seventh inning of Game 3?

1981 Divisional Playoff
Oakland 3 games, Kansas City 0 games

With the players' strike wiping out two months of the season, the Royals were able to rebound from their poor start and, after a change in managers, capture the second half division title. The Oakland A's quickly proved who the division champs were, though, and took out Kansas City in three games.

1. Why was there a divisional playoff in 1981?

2. How many home runs did the Royals hit in the series?

3. How many runs did the Royals score in the series?

4. The Royals lost Game 2, 2-1. Who was the losing pitcher for KC?

5. Who was the losing pitcher for Kansas City in Game 3?

John Wathan argues a point in the '81 Divisional playoff.

1984 ALCS
Detroit 3 games, Kansas City 0 games

Kansas City returned to the ALCS after a three-year absence, but were a little overmatched by the eventual World Champion Detroit Tigers. The Royals played the Tigers tough in Games 2 and 3, but ran out of gas. The team provided a nice sneak peak to next season's club.

1. Who was the Royals' starter in Game 1?

2. Who started Game 2 for KC?

3. Who hit a home run for the Tigers in Game 2?

4. The Royals lost Game 2 in extra innings. Who was the losing pitcher?

5. Who pitched a complete-game three-hitter against the Tigers in Game 3, but lost, 1-0?

6. Who was the Royals' leading hitter in the series?

Detroit's Sparky Anderson and KC's Dick Howser meet before the '84 ALCS.

1985 ALCS
Kansas City 4 games, Toronto 3 games

The difference between us and everyone else is George Brett.
Dane Iorg
Royals' Utility Player

Kansas City pulled off one of the great comebacks in the history of the ALCS, overcoming a three games to one deficit, to beat the Blue Jays for the AL pennant. George Brett led the way with great hitting as the Royals returned to the World Series.

1. He had only four hits in the series for the Royals, but they were a single, double, triple and home run. He also had six RBIs. Who is he?

2. Charlie Leibrandt lost two of the games in the series for the Royals. Who lost the other game?

3. How many saves did Quiz have in the series?

4. Danny Jackson had a complete-game shutout and beat the Blue Jays, 2-0. What other game did he pitch in?

5. How many bases did the Royals steal in the series?

Brett slams one of his many hits against Toronto during the 1985 ALCS.

George Brett and Willie Wilson talk with reporters during the club's post-game celebration. Both players were key figures in the Royals' series win.

6. Who started Games 3 and 7 for KC, but didn't figure in either decision?

7. Who was the winning pitcher in Game 7 for the Royals?

8. Who hit homers in Games 2 and 7 while playing right field for Kansas City?

9. This Toronto pitcher had two of the Blue Jays' three wins, getting both in relief. Who is he?

10. As a team, how many home runs did the Royals hit? And Toronto?

11. How many homers did Brett hit?

12. Who was the series MVP?

Hal McRae is safe at second in the 1985 ALCS.

George Brett and Bret Saberhagen take a break during Game 7 of the 1985 World Series.

The World Series

1980 World Series
Philadelphia 4 games, Kansas City 2 games

I'd be talking to other outfielders between innings and we'd say 'Damn, we just can't hold a lead.'

Willie Wilson
during the 1980 World Series

I thought our players were a little tight there...I thought the World Series atmosphere intimidated them a little bit.

Jim Frey
on Royals playing in Philly

I'm frustrated, but there's nothing I can do about it. The more you move, the more it hurts.

George Brett
on his hemorrhoids

It'll be nice to go home and see somebody friendly, somebody who uses nice four-letter words.

Dan Quisenberry
on the Philadelphia fans

After three near-misses, the Royals finally beat the Yankees and brought the World Series to Kansas City. It proved to be anti-climatic though, as the Royals seemed satisfied with their ALCS win and were happy just to be playing in the Series.

Amos Otis and Willie Aikens starred, and despite one of the most famous cases of hemorrhoids ever, George Brett also supplied some offense. But the pitching was shaky throughout the series, and Philadelphia made the most of the breaks presented to them and captured the championship.

1. Who was the Royals Game 1 starter in Philadelphia?

2. Which Royals player hit a home run in his first World Series at-bat?

3. Which pitcher lost two games to the Phillies in the series?

4. Which Royal had 11 hits and led the team with a .478 batting average for the series?

5. How many home runs did the Royals hit in the series? How many did the Phillies hit?

6. How many stolen bases did the Royals have in the series?

7. Which Royal was thrown out at home twice, once in Game 1, and again in Game 5?

Willie Aikens supplied a lot of power for the Royals in the '80 World Series.

8. Who homered twice in Game 1, and hit two more in Game 4 to set a World Series record for two multi-homer games?

9. Which Royal struck out with the bases loaded in the bottom of the 9th inning to end Game 5?

10. Who was on base for KC during that final strikeout in Game 5?

11. Who was the winning pitcher for the Royals in Game 4?

12. Which Philadelphia starter beat the Royals twice in the series?

13. How many home runs did Brett hit in the series?

14. Which three Royals hit .400 or better for the series?

15. Who had the most RBIs for Kansas City in the series?

16. The Phillies had only three home runs as a team. Who hit them?

Frank White and Clint Hurdle celebrate during Game 5 action.

17. How many RBIs did Hal McRae have for the series?

18. Who made the last out of the series?

Despite his problems, Brett still hit well in the series.

Darryl Motley celebrates as he watches his home run leave the stadium in Game 7 of the 1985 World Series.

1985 World Series
Kansas City 4 games, St. Louis 3 games

Any time you're down 2-0 in a short series, it's never easy. It's tough, but it's been done before. (Not after losing the first two games at home)

Dick Howser
after Game 2

We do have our backs to the wall. We have become friends with our backs to the wall. We know all the crevices.

Dan Quisenberry
after the Royals lost Game 4

Being down and out as much as we were and accomplishing what we did is unbelievable. These are special people. I've been on some great ball clubs in the '70s. This year we were a great ballclub, but this was a little different. This was a great ballclub inside.

George Brett
after winning the
1985 World Series

The improbable finish to an incredible season for the Royals—a World Series Championship! Kansas City completed the greatest season of comebacks by winning the final three games of the 1985 ALCS and then matched that feat by doing it again in the World Series. In the end, Kansas City embarrassed St. Louis with a Game 7 laugher to bring home the championship banner.

After dropping the first two games at home (no team in the history of the series had ever won after losing the first two games at home), the Royals fought back and took two out of three in St. Louis. A controversial call and outstanding pitching put the finishing touches on the comeback at Royals Stadium. Bret Saberhagen was the series star, but George Brett, as always, provided a lot of the offensive punch.

1. Who was the Royals' starter in Game 1?

2. Which Cardinal starter defeated the Royals in Game 1?

Bret Saberhagen receives congratulations from Manager Dick Howser and his teammates after defeating the Cardinals in Game 3.

3. Who was the losing pitcher for Kansas City in Game 2?

4. With the bases loaded in the ninth inning, who got the game-winning hit for the Cardinals that won Game 2?

5. Who was the Royals' cleanup hitter in Game 3?

6. Bret Saberhagen started and won Game 3 for the Royals in St. Louis. Who was the Cardinals' starter?

7. How many former Cardinal players were on the Royals' World Series roster?

8. How many home runs did the Royals hit in the series? How many did the Cardinals hit?

9. How many stolen bases did the Royals have? The Cardinals?

10. Who was the Royals' top hitter in the series?

Game 6 hitting hero Dane Iorg.

Game 6—Safe at First!

Cardinal fans have been whining about this game for more than a decade now, claiming a bad call cost their team a world championship. Nothing could be further from the truth. Shoddy play and an overall lack of composure hurt the Cardinals during the crucial plays that followed the call at first base in the bottom of the 9th inning of Game 6. KC took advantage of the mishaps—as championship teams usually do—and pulled out a thrilling victory to force a Game 7. How much do you remember about what happened during the Royals' game-winning rally?

1. What was the score of Game 6 going into the bottom of the 9th?

2. Who led off for the Royals?

3. Who was pitching for St. Louis?

4. Who fielded the ball and threw to first?

5. Who covered the bag?

6. Who was the first base umpire that made the "controversial" call?

7. Who was the second hitter in the inning, and what happened during his at bat?

8. Who made the only out of the inning for KC?

9. Who was at bat when Cardinal catcher Darrell Porter was charged with a passed ball?

10. Who had the game-winning hit for the Royals, and who was he pinch-hitting for?

11. Who scored the winning run?

12. Who was the winning pitcher?

Safe at First?

11. Who was the Cardinals' top hitter in the series?

12. KC's pitchers held the Cardinals to just 13 runs and the all-time low World Series team batting average, .185, for a seven-game series. What was the Royals' team batting average?

13. Who was the winning pitcher for the Royals in Game 5?

14. The Royals scored three runs in the second inning of Game 5. Who had a two-run triple in that inning?

The Cardinals' Tommy Herr argues his point on the controversial call at first base in Game 6.

Jim Sundberg and Dick Howser confer with Charlie Leibrandt during Game 6.

Jim Sundberg eludes Cardinal catcher Darrell Porter's tag to score the winning run in Game 6. Lonnie Smith and Buddy Biancalana greet the exuberant Sundberg.

15. Who was the Cardinals' starter in Game 7?

16. How many pitchers did St. Louis use in Game 7?

17. Saberhagen pitched his second complete game of the series in Game 7. How many hits did he give up?

Dan Quisenberry pitched big in Game 6 for Kansas City.

Danny Jackson pitches during Game 1 of the 1985 World Series at Royals Stadium.

18. How many strikeouts did Saberhagen have in Game 7?

19. This player hit a two-run home run in the second inning to put KC ahead in Game 7. Who was he?

20. Who caught the last out of the Game 7?

21. Who was the series MVP?

22. Two Cardinals were ejected in the fifth inning of Game 7. Who were they?

Stadiums

The Royals have called two different stadiums home since the franchise entered the American League in 1969. Municipal Stadium, the club's first ballpark, never seemed a part of the club, especially since the new sports complex was under construction before the team played its first game. When the club started playing in Kauffman Stadium, Kansas City got more than just a new ballpark, it got its first winning team ever in the Major Leagues.

Municipal Stadium

1. How many years did the Royals play at Municipal Stadium?

2. What was the stadium's original name?

3. What other names did the stadium go by before it was called Municipal Stadium? What teams played there?

Municipal Stadium

Opening Day for the Monarchs, May 24, 1953. This is two years before the second deck was added.

4. Where was it located?

5. What was the distance down the left field line when the Royals played there?

6. What was the distance to center field?

7. What was the distance to right field?

8. When did the Royals play their last game there?

Kauffman Stadium

1. What year did the Royals began playing in Kauffman Stadium?

2. What was its original name?

3. What year did the name change?

4. At the time of its opening, how many other American League stadiums had artificial turf?

5. Which Royals' player hit the first home run in Kauffman Stadium?

6. Who threw the first no-hitter in Kauffman Stadium? When?

7. What were the original distances to the left, center and right field walls?

8. The distances to the outfield fences have been changed twice at Kauffman Stadium. When were they changed?

9. What year was real grass installed at Kauffman Stadium?

10. How much did the Kauffman Stadium renovation cost?

11. What year was the renovation completed?

12. What is the seating capacity for "The New K?"

Kauffman Stadium

**1970-71
Road Uniform**

**Home Uniform for 1970s
and early 1980s**

**Road Uniform for 1970s
and early 1980s**

Uniforms

Knowing Kansas City's baseball fans might shy away from flash, odd color combinations, and trend-breaking designs, Royals management opted for the conventional when it came to their new team's uniforms. The other 1969 expansion teams (Pilots, Padres, and Expos) chose "modern" designs and colors, but the Royals' new uniforms were classic in both color and design—a far cry from the green and gold of their departed predecessor, the A's.

With just a few variances over the years—primarily polyester pullovers and elastic waist bands—the Royals have maintained a classic look on the field of play.

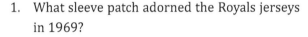

1. What sleeve patch adorned the Royals jerseys in 1969?

1985 Home Uniform

2. What year did the team logo sleeve patch first appear on the jerseys?

3. When did the Royals switch to polyester pullover jerseys?

4. What year did players' names first adorn the back of the jerseys?

5. What year did the team return to buttoned jerseys?

6. What was on the front of the Royals' first road jersey (1969)?

7. The Royals have worn another team's uniform on several different occasions. Which team uniform did they wear and why?

1972 Road Uniform

193

8. In 1983, the Royals made a change to the front of their road jerseys. What was it?

9. An alternate blue jersey was introduced by the club in 1994. What specific guidelines did the team have for wearing the jersey?

10. An alternate cap was introduced and worn during the 1995 season. When did the team wear the cap?

11. In 2002, the Royals added another color to their uniforms. What was that color?

12. The Royals had two alternate jerseys in the early 2000s. What color were the jerseys?

13. The Royals wore a vest jersey for a few years. What year did they first wear a vest jersey?

14. What year did the Royals start wearing an alternate light blue jersey at home?

Alternate Jersey

1990s Road Uniform

1980s Road Uniform

1969 Home Uniform

Uniform Numbers

1. What number did George Brett first wear with the Royals?

2. What number did Amos Otis wear?

3. What number did Hal McRae wear?

4. What number did Brian McRae wear?

5. What number did Paul Splittorff wear?

6. What number did Dennis Leonard wear?

7. What number did Danny Tartabull wear?

8. What number did John Mayberry wear?

9. What was Bret Saberhagen's first uniform number?

10. What number did Saberhagen change to?

11. What number did Dan Quisenberry wear?

12. What was the first uniform number Alex Gordon wore?

13. What was Carlos Beltran's first uniform number with the Royals?

14. What is Billy Butler's uniform number?

15. What number did Zack Greinke wear?

16. What was the first uniform number Johnny Damon wore with the Royals?

George Brett expresses his point of view after being called out for having too much pine tar on his bat in the infamous Pine Tar Game. His home run, which put the Royals ahead of the Yankees, 5-4, was instead called an out, ending the game. The Royals protested to the American League office and the final inning was later played out from the point following Brett's home run.

The Pine Tar Game

Despite everything he achieved throughout his career, George Brett will always be remembered more for the "Pine Tar Game" than any other single game or award. His liberal use of pine tar to enhance the feel of his bat not only led to the eventual rewriting of the rule book, but gave baseball one of its more outrageous—and memorable—moments. The fact it was New York and Kansas City, as well as George Brett, made the home run, original game-ending sequence, and preposterous replay finish even more memorable.

How much do you know about the game?

1. When (original date) and where did the Pine Tar Game take place?

2. Who was the manager of the Yankees?

3. When Brett hit the Pine Tar home run, what was the score of the game, and who was on base?

4. Who was the umpire that made the Pine Tar call?

5. What three rules did the umpires use to disallow Brett's home run?

6. The American League President upheld the Royals' protest and reversed the call, counting the home run. Who was he, and why did he reverse the call?

7. On what date was the game resumed?

8. Who was the losing pitcher for New York?

9. Who was the winning pitcher in the game for the Royals?

10. Who finished the game for the Royals?

11. Who finished the game for the Yankees?

12. Who made the final out in the Royals' 9th inning?

13. Who were the batters in the Yankees' half of the 9th inning?

Speed

The Royals have always been associated with speed. Stolen bases and aggressive base running were an integral part of the team's offense throughout the club's glory years in the 1970s and 1980s. Double steals, hit and runs, taking the extra base—Kansas City played an exciting style of baseball, and speed was a big part of the club's winning tradition.

1. How many Royals have led the league in stolen bases, who are they, and how many bases did they steal?

2. How many times have the Royals led the American League in stolen bases, and in what years?

Willie Wilson slides in safely for one of his many stolen bases.

Amos Otis eludes a tag for another stolen base.

3. Who was the first Royal to steal a base?

4. Who was the first Royal to steal a base in Kauffman Stadium?

5. Who was the first Royal to steal home?

6. How many times did George Brett steal home in his career?

7. Who has stolen home the most times in Royals history, and how many times?

8. John Wathan set a stolen base record in 1982. What was it?

9. Whose record did Wathan break?

10. Who holds the Royals' team record for the most career stolen bases? How many?

11. This Royals' outfielder finished second in the AL in stolen bases in 1995 and 1996. Who was he, and how many bases did he steal?

George Brett wasn't the fastest of Royals, but he was smart on the base-paths, and always ready to take an extra base or steal in a key situation. Here he slides in safely for a double against the Yankees.

12. The Royals' team record for stolen bases is 218. What year did they steal this amount?

13. This speedy outfielder came to the Royals from the New York Mets and is just one of five Royals' players to steal 50 or more bases in a season. Who is he?

14. This outfielder stole more than 50 bases in a season twice, in 1995 and 1996. Who is he?

15. Who was the last Royals' player to lead the league in stolen bases?

16. The Royals' team record for triples in a season is 79. What year did the Royals set this record?

17. What is the team record for stolen bases in a game?

Nicknames

What's in a name? The Royals have had a few players with memorable nicknames over the years, and a few with some you've probably never heard before. Here's a sampling of both.

1. Who was called "Mullet?"

2. Two different Royals were called "Opie." Who were they?

3. Which pitcher was called "Big Man?"

4. What was Danny Jackson's nickname?

5. Freddie Patek had two nicknames. What were they?

6. What is Bo Jackson's real first name?

7. Who was called "Sweetstick?"

8. "The Duke." Who is he?

9. What was Jim Sundberg's nickname?

10. What is Cookie Rojas' real name?

11. Who is "Bye-Bye?"

12. Who was called "Duck", and why?

13. Who was called "Spider?"

14. What is Whitey Herzog's real name?

15. Who was "Mr. Ribbie?"

16. What was Joe Randa's nickname?

17. What Royals' pitcher was called "Flash?"

18. Who was the "Mexicutioner?"

19. What was Jeff Suppan's nickname?

Game 7, 1985 World Series. Darryl Motley connects for one of the biggest home runs in the history of the Royals.

Home Runs

Home runs have never been a major offensive weapon for the Royals, but there have been a few memorable ones hit by the team, and you could even say there were a few sluggers in their lineup over the years.

1. Who hit the first home run in Royals' history?

2. Who hit the first grand slam in team history?

3. Who holds the Royals' record for the most home runs in a season, and how many did he hit?

4. Who is the only Royals' player to homer in his first official Major League at-bat?

5. Only one Royals' player has ever hit three home runs in a doubleheader. Who is he?

6. Who hit the first pinch-hit home run in Royals' history?

7. Only one Royals' player has ever hit three home runs in a game at Kauffman Stadium. Who is he, and when did he do it?

8. How many Royals have hit 30 or more home runs in a season? Who are they, and how many did they hit?

9. George Brett holds the Royals' record for career home runs. How many did he hit?

10. Who is second in career home runs for the Royals?

11. How many career home runs did John Mayberry hit with the Royals?

12. How many home runs did Danny Tartabull hit with KC?

13. In 1988, one player hit three grand slams. Who was that player?

14. In 2010, this infielder hit three grand slams. Who was he?

15. Who was the last Royal to hit at least 30 home runs in a season?

16. Who hit the first walk-off home run in Royals' history?

Miscellaneous

1. Who was the first player selected by the Royals in the expansion draft on October 15, 1968?

2. The Royals have only defeated one opponent in every contest played during an entire season. Who was that opponent?

3. Who holds the club record for consecutive games played?

4. What is the longest game (innings) in Royals' history?

5. What are the most hits recorded by the Royals in a game?

6. What is the largest shutout victory in Royals' history?

7. Which two players hold the club record for hits in a game?

8. What is the largest winning margin in Royals' history?

9. Who holds the club record for home runs by a left-handed batter in a season?

10. Ewing Kauffman sold 49 percent of the Royals in 1983. Who did he sell to?

11. When did Kauffman regain full ownership of the Royals?

12. Brian McRae was a first-round draft pick in what year?

13. When did the Royals tour Japan?

14. Who comprised the Royals' first radio broadcast team?

15. How many All Star games have been played at Kauffman Stadium? When?

16. What year did the David Glass Family purchase the Royals?

17. How many times have the Royals lost 100 games or more in a season?

18. How many times have the Royals finished in last place in their division?

19. The Royals have had the first overall pick in the amateur draft once. When did they have the pick, and who did they select?

20. In what year did the Royals record their lowest team ERA?

The Answers

Royals Players Trivia

George Brett
1. El Segundo High (California)
2. He singled off Stan Bahnsen
3. Ferguson Jenkins on May 8, 1974, at Texas
4. Three. 1975 with 13 (tied for 1st), 1976 with 14 and 1979 with 20
5. Twice, with 45 in both 1978 and 1990
6. 1976 and 1979
7. 1987
8. He singled off Chicago's Joel Davis at Royals Stadium on May 25, 1986
9. California's Tim Fortugno at Anaheim
10. He was picked off first base
11. One, September 28, 1980, against Minnesota. It was a grand slam.
12. Jon Matlack
13. August 29, 1982, at Comiskey Park in Chicago. It was a single off Lamar Hoyt.
14. The Indians' Mark Clark on May 13, 1993, at Cleveland
15. Stan Musial, Hank Aaron, Willie Mays, Al Kaline and Carl Yastrzemski
16. Mitch Williams of the Rangers on June 1. It was also his 1,000th RBI.
17. The Indians' Mark Clark at Cleveland
18. 13 (1976-1988)
19. 11 consecutive (1976-1986)
20. Twice
21. 1980 and 1981
22. 3,154 hits
23. Tom Henke of the Texas Rangers at Arlington Stadium
24. 2,707 games
25. .305
26. Nolan Ryan & Robin Yount

Hal McRae
1. Florida A&M
2. July 11, 1968, with the Reds
3. 1977 (54) and 1982 (46)
4. Once, 1982 with 133 RBI
5. 2,091
6. Wayne Simpson came with Hal McRae to the Royals from Reds on November 30, 1972. Roger Nelson and Richie Schienblum went to Cincinnati.
7. Hitting coach

8. .332
9. Seven (1974-76, 1982-84, 1987)
10. None
11. .000 (no hits in one official at bat, with one walk)
12. .400 (18 for 45)

Frank White
1. June 12, 1973 at Baltimore
2. Shortstop
3. June 14; a single off the Orioles' Doyle Alexander
4. June 27 at Oakland
5. April 6, 1974 (Opening Day) off Minnesota's Tom Burgmeier
6. Eight
7. 1977
8. Six (1977-1982)
9. 1978
10. Five
11. 1979
12. 2,006

Willie Wilson
1. September 4, 1976, against Texas at Royals Stadium
2. Once, with 83 in 1979
3. 21 in 1985
4. Gary Templeton
5. First major leaguer to have 700 official at bats
6. Five times (1980, 1982, 1985, 1987, 1988)
7. Once, with 133 in 1980
8. One, with a batting average of .332 in 1982
9. Two, 1982 and 1983
10. Three
11. The Oakland Athletics and the Chicago Cubs

Bret Saberhagen
1. Cleveland High in Reseda, California
2. True
3. Shortstop
4. 19th
5. April 4, 1984, against the Yankees at Royals Stadium. He gave up three hits in 4.2 innings as the Royals lost, 4-3.

6. 19 years, 11 months and 24 days
7. Detroit on April 19, 1984. He beat the Tigers 5-2.
8. He was traded to the New York Mets with Bill Pecota for Greg Jefferies, Keith Miller and Kevin McReynolds.
9. Two
10. 110
11. True. He is the only Royals pitcher to win the fielding award.
12. August 26, 1991 against the White Sox at Royals Stadium

Bo Jackson

1. Steve Carlton of the White Sox
2. Mike Moore, September 14, 1986, at Royals Stadium
3. Bo led the American League in strikeouts with 172 in 1989.
4. No, he never won a Gold Glove.
5. He was the first 25-25 Royal in the club's history (25 HRs and 27 SBs).
6. 1984
7. 34
8. Randy Johnson of Seattle
9. 1989
10. Rick Reuschel of the Giants
11. Homer and steal a base

Amos Otis

1. New York Mets
2. Otis came to the Royals in a trade with Bob Johnson from the Mets for Joe Foy.
3. 1971
4. Fred Patek
5. 1973
6. Five
7. He stole five bases in one game against Milwaukee.
8. 1971
9. Three
10. Pittsburgh

Dan Quisenberry

1. July 8, 1979 against Chicago at Royals Stadium. KC lost, 4-2.
2. July 23, 1979, at Texas. He worked .1 inning in a 5-4 KC win.
3. Five (1980, 1982-85)
4. Had 40 or more saves two years in a row (45 in '83, 44 in '84)
5. Three – Laverne College (California), Orange Coast College (California, Junior

College), and Pacific College (Fresno, California)
6. Three (1982-84)
7. No. He stared one game in the minors, for Waterloo, IA in 1975, a complete game victory, 5-3.
8. St. Louis and San Francisco
9. 573
10. Three (1980, 1983, and 1985)

Steve Busby

1. USC, where he led the Trojans to the national title in 1971.
2. September 8, 1972 against Minnesota. Steve won the game, 3-2.
3. Two, 1974 and 1975
4. Twice, 1973 and 1975
5. AL Rookie Pitcher of the Year
6. He threw a no-hitter
7. April 27, 1973, at Tiger Stadium; June 19, 1974, at Milwaukee's County Stadium
8. 70
9. None
10. 13, at Milwaukee, July 10, 1973

Dennis Leonard

1. He was their second-round pick in the 1972 June free-agent draft
2. Oceanside High School (New York)
3. Iona College
4. September 4, 1975
5. Three
6. 106
7. He tied Nolan Ryan of California and Mike Flannagan of Baltimore with five shutouts.
8. 1977
9. Innings pitched, 201
10. 1978, 1979, 1980

Cookie Rojas

1. The Reds
2. Sandy Koufax
3. Four
4. The Phillies, 1965
5. One. A home run at Atlanta in the 1972 game.
6. Twice. 1965 (.303) with Philadelphia and 1971 (.300) with the Royals
7. Kansas City acquired Cookie from the Cardinals on June 13, 1970, for Fred Rico.

8. Luis Alcarez was the Royals' Opening Day second baseman in 1970.
9. The California Angels

Fred Patek
1. The Pirates
2. Jerry May and Bruce Dal Canton
3. 5'5" – He was the smallest man in major league baseball during his career.
4. Once. He had 53 in 1977 to lead the league.
5. False. He led the league once with 11 in 1971.
6. Two (1976 and 1978)
7. The Angels
8. Jim Perry
9. 385
10. .242

John Mayberry
1. The Astros. Kansas City sent Lance Clemmons and Jim York to Houston for Mayberry and Dave Grangaard on December 2, 1971.
2. Walks. He had 122 in 1973; 119 in 1975.
3. Twice, in 1973 and 1974
4. 143
5. One, in Game 5.
6. Twice. He did on July 1, 1975, at Texas, and again on June 1, 1977, at Toronto.
7. 1973, .420
8. Fred Lynn of the Red Sox.
9. .253
10. The New York Yankees

Larry Gura
1. Arizona State
2. Tulsa
3. The Cubs and Yankees
4. Fran Healy
5. Eighteen. He did it twice, in 1980 and 1982
6. The Cubs
7. None. He started two games but had no decisions
8. One, in 1980
9. 2.19, best for the series
10. One, four times (1970, 1971, 1976, 1985)

Jeff Montgomery
1. Marshall University, where he earned a degree in Computer Science
2. From the Reds in a trade for Van Snider

in 1987
3. June 4, 1988
4. One, with the Reds in 1987
5. June 8, 1988 against Oakland
6. 1993
7. Three – 1992, 1993, 1996
8. 304
9. 46

Kevin Appier
1. Fresno State University and Antelope Valley J.C.
2. He was selected in the first round of the 1987 June draft (ninth pick overall)
3. June 4, 1989 at California
4. June 13, 1989. He pitched five innings against the A's as the Royals won, 5-3.
5. June 15, 1997. He beat the Pirates 8-1 at Pittsburgh.
6. Once, 1995.
7. 2.56
8. Six, 1992-1997.
9. Once. He had 207 in 1996.
10. He struck out four batters in one inning on September 3, 1996 in Toronto. He K'd Ed Sprague, Carlos Delgado, Charlie O'Brien, and Alex Gonzalez (Delgado reached first on a wild pitch).

Paul Splittorff
1. Morningside College, where he earned a Bachelor of Science in Business Administration
2. September 23, 1970
3. June 8, 1971. He beat the Senators in Kansas City, 4-2.
4. 1973. His record was 20-11.
5. 166 wins
6. 143 losses
7. 1,057, fifth all-time for the Royals
8. 2-0. He beat the Yankees in 1976 and 1977
9. Three
10. True.

Alex Gordon
1. Third base, first base, and left field
2. Lincoln Southeast High School in Lincoln, NE
3. The University of Nebraska
4. He struck out with the bases loaded.
5. Three—2011, 2012 and 2013
6. Topps issued his rookie card prematurely in 2006 before he made the 25 man

roster or had played in one major league game. They stopped producing them, but some made their way to retail stores and have become highly collectible.
7. 2013 as outfielder
8. He started the season on a minor league rehab assignment with the Class-A Advanced league team Wilmington after he suffered a broken thumb in spring training.
9. He led with assists—20.
10. He led the majors in doubles with 51.

Billy Butler
1. May 1, 2007
2. He singled.
3. University of Florida, but he decided to go pro and did not attend.
4. William Raymond Butler, Jr.
5. Besides his exemplary play on the field, he and his wife started the Hit-It-A-Ton campaign in 2008 to help feed disadvantaged families in the Kansas City area. Butler donates $250 for each of his HRs and $125 for each of his doubles.
6. He was selected for the All-Star Game. He also received the Silver Slugger Award and the Edgar Martinez Outstanding Designated Hitter Award.
7. He hit the go-ahead home run and was voted MVP of the game.
8. With the Idaho Falls Chukars which is a Pioneer League affiliate of the Royals.
9. Wolfson High School in Jacksonville, Florida
10. He was the 14th overall pick by the Royals in the first round of 2004 draft.
11. Country Breakfast

Mark Gubicza
1. William Penn Charter High School in Philadelphia
2. April 6, 1984 against Cleveland. He lost the game, 2-0.
3. May 12, 1984 against Boston. He pitched a four-hit shutout, winning 4-0.
4. 132
5. Two, 1988 and 1989
6. None
7. 1988. He was 20-8 for the season.
8. 14 K's against the Twins on August 27, 1988
9. Frank Viola and Dennis Eckersley

Mike Sweeney
1. August 12, 1996. He hit it off Seattle Mariner pitcher, Jamie Moyer. It was a three-run homer.
2. The two lead the league in most frequently hit batters, each 15 times.
3. He hit a grand slam on July 22, 2004 and then hit a three-run homer later in the game for a total of seven RBI's.
4. His first major league hit was a single. He got it as a pinch hitter off Paul Assenmacher at Cleveland's Jacobs Field in the final game of the 1995 season.
5. 3 teams besides the Royals, Oakland A's, Seattle Mariners and Philadelphia Phillies.
6. Catcher
7. Five. 2000, 2001, 2002, 2003 and 2005
8. 2003-2007
9. He was drafted just out of Ontario High School in Ontario, California just before his 18th birthday.
10. He was given a standing ovation each time he came to bat.

Carlos Beltran
1. Puerto Rico
2. 1998
3. Golden Spikes
4. none
5. none
6. four times (1999, 2001, 2002, 2003)
7. Fred Garcia, pitcher with the Mariners
8. 26

More Trivia

Ewing Kauffman
1. 1968
2. Garden City, Missouri
3. Navy
4. 1950
5. 1973
6. July 2, 1993
7. The Board of Directors

Pitchers
1. Tom Gordon
2. Dennis Leonard
3. Bret Saberhagen, 20 years and 8 days old when he started at Detroit on April 19, 1984
4. Kevin Appier. He struck out four batters in one inning on September 3, 1996 in Toronto. He K'd Ed Sprague, Carlos Delgado, Charlie O'Brien and Alex Gonzalez (Delgado reached first on a wild pitch).
5. Bret Saberhagen
6. Rich Gale won 11 games in a row in 1980
7. Paul Splittorff in 1973
8. Al Fitzmorris
9. Dennis Leonard
10. Ted Abernathy
11. Dennis Leonard with 40
12. Bob Johnson with 206 in 1970, Dennis Leonard with 244 in 1977, and Kevin Appier with 207 in 1996.
13. No
14. Bret Saberhagen, 2.16 in 1989
15. Paul Splittorff, 19 in 1974
16. Roger Nelson
17. Splittorff with 144, Gubizca with 135 and Leonard with 106
18. Kevin Appier
19. Bret Saberhagen, 1989
20. Wally Bunker
21. Saberhagen in 1985 and 1989, David Cone in 1994, Zack Greinke in 2009
22. Mark Davis
23. Gaylord Perry, 1983
24. Al Hrabosky
25. Jeremy Guthrie, from Aug. 8, 2012, to May 9, 2013.
26. Greg Holland, 47; Jeff Montgomery, 45; Dan Quisenberry, 45 and 44; Joakim Soria, 43 and 42.
27. Jose Rosado
28. Darrell May
29. Zack Greinke with 15 against Cleveland on Aug. 25, 2009.
30. Larry Gura on May 21, 1980 against Oakland.

Catchers
1. Buck Martinez
2. Milwaukee
3. Bob Boone, 1989
4. John Wathan
5. Ellie Rodriguez
6. Darrell Porter, with 112 in 1977
7. Boston
8. Brent Mayne
9. Darrell Porter
10. Ed Hearn
11. Fran Healy
12. Gregg Zaun, Hector Ortiz, Brian Johnson, and Jorge Fabregas
13. John Buck
14. The Texas Rangers
15. Miguel Olivo
16. Jason Kendall
17. one

First Basemen
1. Chuck Harrison
2. Steve Balboni
3. California
4. Bob Oliver
5. John Wathan
6. Clint Hurdle
7. San Diego
8. Willie Aikens
9. Houston
10. Bob Hamelin
11. Pete LaCock
12. Kevin Seitzer
13. Toronto
14. John Mayberry, George Brett, Mike Sweeney, and Ken Harvey
15. Ross Gload

Second Basemen
1. Jerry Adair
2. Cookie Rojas
3. Fifteen, 1976-1990
4. Terry Shumpert
5. Dave Nelson
6. Keith Lockhart
7. The Angels and White Sox
8. Keith Miller
9. U.L. Washington
10. Mark Grudzielanek
11. Ruben Gotay, Tony Graffanino, Wilton Guerrero, Damian Jackson, Mendy Lopez, Donnie Murphy, Desi Relaford
12. Carlos Febles
13. Mike Aviles
14. Chris Getz

Third Basemen

1. Joe Foy
2. Bob Oliver
3. Paul Schaal
4. 1974. He took over from Paul Schaal after the season started.
5. Kevin Seitzer
6. Greg Pryor
7. Gary Gaetti
8. Gary Gaetti
9. Texas
10. One, Brett in 1985
11. Detroit
12. Mark Teahen
13. Mark Teahen
14. Mike Moustakas

Shortstops

1. Jackie Hernandez
2. Eight. 1971, 1973-1979
3. U.L. Washington
4. Onix Concepcion and Buddy Biancalana
5. Angel Salazar
6. Danny Jackson
7. Bob Floyd
8. Greg Gagne
9. David Howard
10. Montreal and Pittsburgh
11. Frank White
12. Lance Mulliniks
13. Jackie Hernandez, Rich Severson and Tom Matchick
14. George Brett
15. none
16. Angel Berroa
17. The Milwaukee Brewers

Outfielders

1. Ed Kirkpatrick in left, Lou Piniella in center and Bob Oliver in right
2. Seattle Pilots
3. Vada Pinson
4. Jim Wohlford
5. Al Cowens
6. Tom Poquette
7. Three. Amos Otis (1971, 1973-74), Al Cowens (1977) and Willie Wilson (1980)
8. Joe Zdeb
9. Clint Hurdle
10. Lonnie Smith
11. Scott Bankhead, Mike Kingery and Steve Shields
12. Jerry Martin
13. Al Cowens

14. Danny Tartabull
15. Vince Coleman. He had 50 steals in 1994
16. Pat Sheridan
17. Alex Gordon
18. Jeff Francouer 2011, Alex Gordon 2012
19. Johnny Damon with 136 in 2000
20. David DeJesus
21. Alex Gordon in 2013

Designated Hitters

1. Ed Kirkpatrick
2. Thirteen
3. Harmon Killebrew
4. Dave Nelson
5. Jorge Orta
6. Left and right field
7. Three (1976, 1980 and 1982)
8. First base
9. Orlando Cepeda
10. Lonnie Smith
11. Mike Jacobs
12. Jose Guillen
13. Eric Hosmer

Managers

1. 16
2. Joe Gordon
3. Jim Frey
4. Charlie Metro
5. Three. John Wathan, Hal McRae and Bob Boone
6. Dick Howser
7. Dick Howser, 1981-1986. Tony Muser is second.
8. Hokkaido Nippon-Ham Fighters
9. Whitey Herzog, .574 (410 wins, 304 losses)
10. Tony Muser with 431
11. Whitey Herzog, Jim Frey and Dick Howser
12. They won 31 and lost 48
13. Tony Pena and Ned Yost
14. Billy Gardner

American League Championship Series

1976 ALCS
1. Mayberry and Brett, both in Game 5
2. Larry Gura
3. Dennis Leonard
4. Doug Bird
5. George Brett, .444
6. Hal McRae
7. Al Cowens and Jim Wohlford
8. Mark Littell
9. Five

1977 ALCS
1. Splittorff
2. McRae, Mayberry and Cowens
3. None
4. Andy Hassler
5. Leonard
6. Fred Patek
7. Dennis Leonard
8. Hal McRae
9. Reggie Jackson
10. Patek. He grounded into a game-ending double play

1978 ALCS
1. Boston, 5-4
2. Larry Gura
3. Catfish Hunter
4. Thurman Munson
5. Fred Patek
6. Dennis Leonard

1980 ALCS
1. Larry Gura
2. George Brett
3. Dennis Leonard
4. Willie Randolph
5. One, in Game 3
6. Dan Quisenberry
7. One, for Leonard in Game 2
8. Willie Wilson and U.L. Washington

1981 Divisional Playoff
1. Because of the strike, the season was divided into two halves
2. None. The A's swept them, 3-0
3. Two
4. Mike Jones
5. Larry Gura

1984 ALCS
1. Buddy Black
2. Bret Saberhagen
3. Kirk Gibson
4. Dan Quisenberry
5. Charlie Leibrandt
6. Don Slaught, .364

1985 ALCS
1. Jim Sundberg
2. Dan Quisenberry
3. One, Game 6
4. Game 1, he pitched one inning of relief
5. Two. Willie Wilson and Lonnie Smith had one each
6. Bret Saberhagen
7. Charlie Leibrandt
8. Pat Sheridan
9. Tom Henke
10. KC had 7, Toronto had 2
11. Three
12. Brett. He hit .348 for the series and had three HRs and five RBIs

The World Series

1980 World Series
1. Dennis Leonard
2. Amos Otis
3. Dan Quisenberry
4. Amos Otis
5. KC had eight, Philly had three
6. Six
7. Darrell Porter
8. Willie Aikens
9. Jose Cardenal
10. Frank White was on third, Hal McRae was on second and Amos Otis was on first. The Phillies won the game, 4-3.
11. Dennis Leonard
12. Steve Carlton, who won Games 2 and 6
13. One, in Game 3
14. Otis, .478; Hurdle, .417; Aikens, .400
15. Aikens with eight
16. Mike Schmidt had two, Bake McBride had one
17. One
18. Willie Wilson struck out, his 12th of the series—a record

1985 World Series

1. Danny Jackson
2. John Tudor
3. Leibrandt
4. Terry Pendleton
5. Frank White
6. Joaquin Andujar
7. Three. Lonnie Smith, Dane Iorg and Jamie Quick
8. Each team hit two home runs
9. Royals had seven, the Cards had two
10. Brett hit .370, Wilson hit .367
11. Tito Landrum hit .360
12. .288
13. Danny Jackson
14. Willie Wilson
15. John Tudor
16. Seven
17. Five
18. He had two strikeouts
19. Daryl Motley
20. Motley
21. Saberhagen
22. Herzog and Andujar

Game 6—Safe at First!

1. 1-0, St. Louis
2. Jorge Orta
3. Todd Worrell
4. Jack Clark
5. Worrell
6. Don Denkinger
7. Steve Balboni. Jack Clark let a pop foul drop. Steve then singled.
8. Sundberg bunted and Orta was forced out at third base
9. McRae
10. Dane Iorg hit for Quisenberry
11. Jim Sundberg
12. Dan Quisenberry

Stadiums

Municipal Stadium

1. Four
2. Muehlbach Stadium
3. Ruppert Stadium and Blues Stadium. The Blues and Monarchs
4. 22nd and Brooklyn in Kansas City, MO
5. 369 feet

6. 421 feet
7. 338 feet
8. October 4, 1972. Kansas City beat Texas, 4-0.

Kauffman Stadium

1. 1973
2. Royals Stadium
3. 1993
4. None
5. John Mayberry, on April 10, 1973
6. Nolan Ryan, then with the Angels, on May 15, 1973. It was the first of his career.
7. 330 feet down the lines and 405 feet to center field
8. 1980 and 1995
9. 1995
10. 250 million dollars
11. It was completed in time for the 2009 season
12. 37,903

Uniforms

1. Major league baseball's 100th anniversary patch
2. 1970
3. 1973
4. 1978
5. 1983
6. Kansas City in script lettering
7. The Kansas City Monarchs, to honor the Negro Leagues
8. Royals appeared on the front of the jerseys instead of Kansas City
9. Home Sunday games
10. On the road
11. Black
12. Blue and Black
13. 2002 for the gray road jersey. They wore a vest jersey at home the next season.
14. 2008

Uniform Numbers
1. 25
2. 26
3. 11
4. 56
5. 34
6. 22
7. 4
8. 7
9. 31
10. 18
11. 29
12. 7
13. 36
14. 16
15. 23
16. 51

The Pine Tar Game
1. July 24, 1983, at Yankee Stadium
2. Billy Martin
3. New York in the lead, 4 to 3. U.L. Washington
4. Tim McClelland, home plate
5. Rules 1.10 (b), 6.06 (d) and 2.00. Since the Pine Tar game, 1.10 (b) in essence became 1.10 (c), and a provision was added to the rule stating that a bat with too much of a grip enhancing substance was not grounds for calling a batter out.
6. Lee McPhail. He said the pine tar on Brett's bat was not a distance enhancing substance and therefore the home run was allowed.
7. August 18, 1983, at Yankee Stadium
8. Goose Gossage
9. Mike Armstrong
10. Dan Quisenberry. He picked up his 33rd save of the year
11. George Frazier
12. Hal McRae struck out.
13. Don Mattingly flied to center, Roy Smalley flied out to deep left and Oscar Gamble grounded out to end the game.

Speed
1. Otis (1971-52), Patek (1977-53), Wilson (1979-83)
2. Six times. 1971-130, 1978-216, 1979-207, 1980-185, 1994-140, 1996-195
3. Joe Foy, on April 9, 1969 at Municipal Stadium against the Twins
4. Fred Patek, in the Stadium's first game, April 10, 1973 against the Rangers

5. Amos Otis, at California, July 31, 1972
6. Twice. August 17, 1976, vs. Cleveland and September 14, 1987, vs. California
7. Jon Nunnally, four times, all in 1995
8. He set the record for most stolen bases by a catcher in the major leagues with 36 thefts.
9. Ray Schalk of the Chicago White Sox
10. Willie Wilson, 612 (with the Royals)
11. Tom Goodwin, 50 in '95 and 66 in '96
12. 1978
13. Vince Coleman. He stole 50 bases in 1994
14. Tom Goodwin, 50 in 1995, 66 in 1996.
15. Johnny Damon with 46 in 2000
16. 1979
17. 8, against Baltimore, Aug. 1, 1998

Home Runs
1. Mike Fiore hit a solo shot at Oakland on April 13, 1969
2. Bob Oliver on July 4, 1969 against Seattle
3. Steve Balboni, 36 in 1985
4. Jon Nunnally
5. Bill Pecota hit three homers in a double-header against the Yankees in 1989
6. Bob Taylor at Detroit, May 6, 1969
7. Danny Tartabull against Oakland on July 6, 1991
8. Eight. Steve Balboni, 36, 1985; Gary Gaetti, 35, 1995; John Mayberry, 34, 1975; Danny Tartabull, 34, 1987 and 31, 1991; Dean Palmer, 34, 1998; Bo Jackson, 32, 1989; George Brett, 30, 1985; Chili Davis, 30, 1997.
9. 317
10. Amos Otis with 193
11. 143, from 1972 through 1977
12. 124, from 1987 through 1991
13. Danny Tartabull
14. Yuniesky Betancourt
15. Jermaine Dye, 33 in 2000
16. Lou Piniella, on June 30, 1969. The Royals defeated the Angels 2-1.

Nicknames
1. George Brett
2. Kurt Stillwell and Jerry Don Gleaton
3. Rich Gale
4. Jason
5. The Flea and Moochie
6. Vincent Edward Jackson
7. U.L. Washington
8. John Wathan
9. Sunny
10. Octavio Rojas
11. Steve Balboni
12. Marty Pattin, for his Donald Duck imitations
13. Roger Nelson
14. Dorrel Norman Elvert Herzog
15. Hal McRae
16. The Joker
17. Tom Gordon
18. Joakim Soria
19. Soup

Miscellaneous
1. Roger Nelson
2. Baltimore Orioles in 1988
3. Hal McRae with 263 games
4. The Royals have played 18-inning games twice, both against the Texas Rangers. KC won 4-3 on June 6, 1991 and lost 4-3 on May 17, 1972
5. 24, at Detroit, June 5, 1976
6. 16-0, against Oakland on June 25, 1984
7. Bob Oliver had six hits against California on May 4, 1969, and Kevin Seitzer had six hits against Boston on August 2, 1987
8. 17 runs. The Royals beat Minnesota, 23-6, on April 6, 1974
9. John Mayberry, with 34 in 1975
10. Avron Fogelman
11. January 1991
12. 1985
13. Following the 1980 World Series
14. Buddy Blattner and Denny Mathews
15. 2, in 1973 and 2012
16. 2000
17. Four times; 2002 - 100 losses, 2004 - 104 losses, 2005 - 106 losses, 2006 - 100 losses
18. 8 times
19. 2006, pitcher Luke Hochevar
20. 1976, 3.21 ERA

Photo Credits

Alan Barzee: 7, 40(a), 57, 59, 61, 62, 63, 64, 65(a), 69, 70, 71, 152, 163, 164, 187(b)

Author's Personal Collection: 8, 13(b), 15, 17, 23, 55, 92, 165, 185

Michael Bodenhamer: 56

George Brace: 13(a), 22(b), 38, 160

Corbis-Bettmann: 2, 34, 36, 172, 196

Kansas City Star: 41, 72, 73, 115

***Lawrence Journal World*, Kansas Collection, University of Kansas Libraries**: 5, 6, 11, 14, 16, 18, 19, 21, 22(a), 24, 25, 26, 28, 29, 30, 31, 33, 37, 39, 40(b), 44, 46, 52, 58, 60, 106, 109, 111, 116, 119, 120, 123, 125, 127, 128, 131, 133, 150, 155, 156, 162, 167, 168, 169, 171, 173, 174, 175, 176, 177(b), 180, 181, 190, 199, 200

National Baseball Hall of Fame: 12, 27, 32, 35, 65(b), 68, 189

Marc Okkonen: 192, 193, 194

Topeka Capital-Journal: 3, 10, 42, 45, 47, 48(b), 49, 50, 51, 52, 53, 54, 102, 112, 177(a), 178, 182, 184, 186, 187(a), 188, 198, 202

USA TODAY Sports: 9, 77, 81, 85, 86, 88, 90, 94, 95, 97, 98, 99, 137, 138, 191

Front cover photo of George Brett: Photo By *USA TODAY Sports*
(c) Copyright *USA TODAY Sports*

Back cover photo of Royals Celebrating: Photo By *USA TODAY Sports*
(c) Copyright *USA TODAY Sports*

About the Author

Mark Stallard has authored more than 12 books, including *Super Chiefs*, *Kansas City Chiefs Encyclopedia* (1st, 2nd, & 3rd editions), and *Tales from the Kansas Jayhawks Locker Room*. *Legacy of Blue* (originally titled *Kansas City Royals Facts & Trivia*) was his first book. He has also written for several publications and newspapers, including *Baseball America* and *The Wichita Eagle*.

Stallard lives in the Kansas City metropolitan area with his wife, Kathleen, and their two sons.

Other Books by Mark Stallard

Super Chiefs
Kansas City Chiefs Encyclopedia (1st, 2nd, & 3rd editions)
Tales from the Kansas Jayhawks Locker Room
Wildcats to Powercats
Then Landry Said to Staubach....
AFL to Arrowhead
Otis Taylor: The Need to Win
Tales from the Jayhawks Gridiron
Echoes of Cincinnati Reds Baseball (Editor)
Echoes of Oklahoma Sooners Football (Editor)
Tales from the Jayhawks Hardwood
Kansas City Royals Facts & Trivia

Mark Stallard Web Sites

http://mstallard76.wix.com/markstallardauthor
http://www.amazon.com/-/e/B001JP2BC0

Made in the USA
Lexington, KY
08 May 2014